Life Unsettled

Life Unsettled

A Scriptural Journey
for Wilderness Times

Cory Driver

Fortress Press

Minneapolis

LIFE UNSETTLED
A Scriptural Journey for Wilderness Times

Cover image: bkirac/iStockphoto.com
Cover design: Alisha Lofgren

Print ISBN: 978-1-5064-6321-6
eBook ISBN: 978-1-5064-6322-3

For Kathy

Even when she is lost and confused,
she still shows us the way

CONTENTS

Introduction

Shortly before I started writing this book, my mother-in-law, Kathy, with whom I have a very close relationship, called me about the 2016 presidential race in the United States. She is conservative in her politics, evangelical in her faith, and cares very deeply about eliminating abortions. As is probably needless to say, my mother-in-law's electoral preferences tend to be Republican.

This phone call with my mother-in-law occurred after the tape of then candidate Donald Trump's "hot mic" conversation with Billy Bush. He was recorded bragging about repeated sexual abuse, not to mention a lack of fidelity. Kathy is nothing if not principled, and she is not one to overlook problems with candidates simply because they are "good" on other issues. In a word, Kathy was stuck. She had to choose between her preference for a candidate who said that he would take action to support her anti-abortion position and her revulsion at the thought of voting for a serial sexual abuser or, at the very least, someone who thought bragging about being a serial sexual abuser was funny. She told me, "Cory, far more than any other time in my adult life, I feel like we as a country are all in the wilderness."

The notion of being in the wilderness that my mother-in-law struggled with is the central concern of this book. This is not a book about politics, though I will address how reading Scripture leads me to think about some political issues. Rather, this is a book about what we do, and what the people of God have done before us, when we find ourselves confronting strange experiences outside of everything normal and comfortable.

When you read the word *wilderness*, what do you imagine? If you are from the American Midwest, as I am, you probably imagine a desert of some sort. That makes sense, as it is the place that we are least familiar with and seems the most removed from our daily lives. In the Bible, the Hebrew word *midbar*, which we translate as "wilderness," specifically implies not a desert but rather simply a place where people do not live or farm. In fact, *midbar* is frequently a good place to drive flocks, because good pasturage for the sheep and goats can be found. Cities, in the Near Eastern world of the Bible, were frequently surrounded by *midbar/* wilderness, where shepherds grazed their flocks. That land was wilderness specifically because it was *not city*. The land does not have to be hostile to be considered wilderness, but it must not be normal, settled life.

In the Greek New Testament, the word *eremos*, which is translated as "wilderness," carries a similar valence, but perhaps even more intensely. The word, whether describing places or people, means something like solitary, lonely, desolate, or deserted. A desert, rain forest, or tropical island in the middle of the ocean each can be described as wilderness by virtue of the lack of human habitation.

What happens, then, when we find ourselves in a wilderness time in our lives? Maybe we have just moved and have not formed our own community yet. Maybe a drastic change has altered our social network, whether we've faced rejection or had to head out on our own in order to make healthy decisions. Maybe we've simply outgrown a community that was perfectly supportive previously but is insufficient for helping us face our current situation. The unsettling wildernesses that we face frequently have more to do with feeling lonely in a crowd than being in some isolated geographic location. In such wildernesses, more often than not, the control that routine, habit, and society exert on our lives and our thinking becomes temporarily weakened, and we can experience the new, novel, strange, and transcendent. If you have ever taken a walk in a forest, gone hiking in the mountains, or been fortunate to find yourself (purposefully and temporarily) on a sparsely populated island, I suspect you probably already have experienced this openness to new ideas and experiences. The reason we take vacations is to get away from normalcy so that we can have time and space to reflect on our routines and whether they are building life in a direction that is positive. Experiencing wilderness can be a good and useful thing.

But what do we do when we find ourselves in the wilderness apart from our own choices, as my mother-in-law did? She felt suddenly alienated from her deeply partisan friends and alone in her discomfort because she wanted to affect policy but was unwilling to disregard the horrifying words of the candidate who seemed most likely to support her policy. She was in an unusual place, unsure of how to proceed and not willing to carry on as if things were normal. Her predicament was an almost perfect definition of a wilderness experience: she was isolated in a moral/ethical place that felt deeply abnormal. The election season and following years have left many of us feeling like we were suddenly living in a wilderness place, a place that is neither familiar nor normal. For me, this was not a new feeling.

My Wilderness Journeys

I was born and grew up in the US Midwest. My family moved every few years because my father worked in the banking industry during the 1980s and '90s, a time of frequent mergers and acquisitions. I remember enjoying moving because it afforded new opportunities to make new friends and learn about new places. I was raised in mainline Protestant traditions. Because we moved frequently, we found our way to different churches, usually Methodist or Pentecostal and very occasionally Lutheran or Catholic. A key experience happened when I was eight years old. I remember begging my parents to let me sit in the pews with them instead of having to go to Sunday school. All I wanted to do was read the Bible and maybe hear some of the sermon. But they thought it was better for me to go to Sunday school to be with kids my own age. I went, reluctantly.

> All I wanted to do was read the Bible and maybe hear some of the sermon.

4

Let me be clear and preclude any fears: my Sunday school teacher did not abuse us in any way. We just were not on the same page, so to speak. I do not know what the other second graders were thinking, but I wanted to learn about God, and so I asked questions about God. I had just moved to the area and had not made any friends yet. I did not have a sense of what the other children were going to do, or not do, so I spoke up. I cannot remember the exact question that I asked about what God is like, but I remember the Sunday school teacher's answer. Our teacher drew the diagram of the three interlocking circles and proceeded to explain that there are some parts of the Trinity that are "just Jesus," "just God," or "just the Spirit"; some parts that are made of two of them overlapping; and some parts that are all three comingled. He said that was all we needed to know.

Probably he just wanted to get back to his planned lesson and for the nerdy new boy to stop asking questions. But I wasn't finished. In fact, I was disgusted. I had been reading the Bible and was hoping that we were going to talk about some of what it said. But instead of a discussion on the character of God, the ruler of the universe, the Messiah, and the Holy Spirit were reduced to interlocking circles, and that was what my teacher wanted me to know about God.

That "lesson" was hard enough to take, but the straw that really broke the camel's back was when we were talking about Noah and about God's love. I was bothered by the lack of attention being paid to almost everyone on earth drowning and what that meant about God's love. My teacher told us that God put Noah in an ark because God loved Noah. I asked why God did not love everyone else. I was told to go sit in the corner because I was "purposefully missing the point." I don't think I was, though. It has always seemed to me that the story of the flood ought to be about, or at least include, the flood.

After being punished for asking questions in Sunday school, I felt like my comfortable, homey church environment had been taken from me. As we moved, one of the few constants was the churches where we children were welcomed, if not always appreciated for being ourselves. But in this new church, it felt like we had plopped down into a spiritual wilderness where I did not know what to think, whom to turn to for answers, or how to get my bearings. I became deeply suspicious of Christians and especially Christian leaders who preached about letting the little children come to Jesus while in practice just trying to keep them contented with crafts, songs, and theological exercises, which in all fairness may have been exactly what my fellow students needed.

With the hubris that only an eight-year-old can possess, I decided that even though I loved God, I was not going to be like one of the anti-intellectual church people I saw around me. I did not want to be Christian if being Christian meant sitting around, singing songs, and listening to a sermon that we would forget by lunch.

I remember consciously choosing to follow God actively (whatever that meant at the time) in my teens. But I was still, and increasingly, deeply suspicious of Christianity and Christians. I soon would get a crash course in other religious traditions.

When the attacks of September 11, 2001, happened during my freshman year of university, I was one of the tens of thousands of Americans to start studying Arabic and comparative religion to better understand our Muslim neighbors. From 1998 to 2002, the number of university students studying Arabic more than doubled, and from 2002 to 2006, the number of institutions of higher education offering Arabic courses rose from 264 to 466.[1] While many of my friends put college on hold to fight in Iraq and Afghanistan (and some never returned), I stayed in school and changed my major. Instead of focusing on prelaw in my quest to be a lawyer, I took all the comparative religion and Middle East studies[2] courses I could. Growing up in the semirural Midwest and never imagining studying, much less preparing to move to, other parts of the world, I was suddenly welcomed into a new, unsettled life for which I was not prepared.

In addition to studying Arabic and Islam, I also studied Hebrew and Judaism formally for the first time. I was preparing to move to Jerusalem to study the Second Intifada's impact on the Israeli tourism economy. I had started taking Hebrew in the year prior to improve my ability to conduct research and basically just survive. Only sixteen months after changing my major and the direction of my life, I flew to Israel to study at the Hebrew University of Jerusalem. This was not a religious endeavor for me at all but purely about studying Southwest Asian political economies and, if I am honest, a bit of budding political Zionism.

While pursuing my official studies and research, I couldn't help but be exposed to rabbinic thought. My Hebrew was still remedial (and almost twenty years later, it still is not excellent), but I was fascinated by religious traditions that not only did not shun questions but welcomed them. The Talmud is famously overflowing with unresolved questions. In a time when I felt deeply uncomfortable with the varieties of Christianity I had grown up with because they avoided open questions or sought to provide the quickest safe answer and then move on, Judaism offered a breath of fresh air for my soul. For the second time in only a few years, the path of my life became unsettled again. Instead of focusing on Southwest Asian politics, I turned to Jewish studies and particularly to rabbinic approaches to the question-raising boundaries of religion, gender, and ethnicity. I took all the Jewish studies courses I could when I returned to the States, planning to go on to graduate school. But once again, I found myself in an unsettled wilderness.

After applying to several schools, I had failed to gain admission to the graduate programs I had applied to, and I was not sure where to go or what to do. On a whim, I decided to join the Peace Corps. Having all my plans fall through was enough for me to experience something of a personal wilderness, but my experience of living in a place outside of regular human settlement would land me in a literal wilderness as well.

The Peace Corps posted me in the interior of Morocco and gave me the task of helping rural women weavers to form government-sponsored cooperatives. For two years, I lived in a rural town in the mountains and had the whole day to do what I wanted. I woke up early, had breakfast with my Arabic-speaking Muslim host father, and then read the Bible for a couple hours. Then I went to "work," which was really just talking with local folks about what kind of businesses they might want to start and encouraging them to go ahead with their plans. While they went for a siesta, I studied and read for a couple more hours before returning to work. Because of all the studying and all my quiet walks to neighboring villages, I had a lot of great time with God. Though I had taken several semesters of Arabic as an undergrad, I was utterly unprepared to speak Moroccan dialectal Arabic, let alone the Tamazight (Berber) that was the mother tongue of most of the people with whom I was to work.

More than language issues, however, I struggled with living in the high desert, which was so different from the towns among the corn and soybean farms of my youth. Every morning, I would sit with my host grandfather, Moha, and he would tell me stories of how he survived his years in the desert, fighting in the Sand War between Morocco and Algerian proxies. For the first several months, these stories were wasted on me, as I only understood every fifth word. Gradually, however, I understood every third word and started to pick up the main ideas of what he was saying.

Eventually, I gleaned much wisdom, such as that when you stop for the night to camp in the desert, you must be sure to orient your sandals in the direction you intend to go the next day in case a sudden sandstorm obscures your destination. Moha told me that the more water you carry, the more you will thirst on your journey. He told me that it is better to drink large amounts of water just before heading out, carry a small amount of water, and firmly resolve before you set out on a journey that you will arrive and not die in the desert. The temptation to quit and lie down may seem attractive, but if you have already decided to live, you will just have to keep going. This would turn out to be good advice for me.

During the next two years, I traipsed all over the Sahara look-ing for villages and villagers with whom to work. Although I was never in serious danger of dying in the desert, I did encounter sandstorms, great thirst, and wild animals (mostly packs of feral dogs) against which I needed to defend myself. As I walked, I often thought, "What am I doing here?" and in my finer moments, "God, what are you doing here?" Not only was I isolated socially from everyone I had ever known to that point, but I also faced being a member of a religious minority for the first time in my life.

I had grown up mostly in mainline Protestant churches and had been particularly active in teaching and leading in the nonde-nominationally specific church I attended during college. Because I had taken Arabic, Hebrew, Jewish studies, and religious studies courses, I thought I was indispensable to the churches I had been serving, but sud-denly, I was the only Christian I knew for miles in the middle of the Sahara in a Muslim country. The churches carried on just fine without me. In rural Morocco, no one was interested in hearing me discuss the importance of Hebrew language for understanding biblical passages, and besides, I had only brought an English-language Bible with me.

> I also faced being a member of a religious minority for the first time in my life.

Mine is an extreme example, but almost all of us have had the experience—frequently after college, during a move, after a breakup, or following a job change—when reality confronts our plans and laughs in our faces. Instead of confidently knowing the way forward in the midst of a well-known and supportive community, suddenly, we are lost, feeling alone and confused. My physical location in a literal wilderness was only of secondary importance to the immense spiritual and social wilderness that I faced. For several months, I had trouble communicating with my new neighbors at all, let alone having the shared vocabulary and emotional bonds to discuss what I was feeling and thinking about God. I was utterly alone, even while surrounded by people. I wasn't sure how God was guiding my path, and I was plagued by yawning uncertainty and confusion. I was sure that after undergrad, I would immediately continue to pursue my academic career. But I had a pile of rejection letters from grad schools seeming to tell me I was wrong. Instead, I ended up in a place that I hadn't planned for and was unprepared to flourish in. I felt lonely, and my surroundings were suddenly disorienting. This is the wilderness so many of us face, no matter where we live or what we do.

Fifteen years later, after three relocations in a year and finally moving into my first house, I am trying to figure out what it means to be a husband, dad, and suburbanite. I feel the same sort of disorientation that I felt in rural Morocco. Who hasn't felt lost and confused when life didn't turn out the way they expected it to? One or two surprising events may happen, and suddenly we are facing a life unsettled. And in this kind of wilderness, when we are in a lonely period, no matter if we are in a crowd or literally alone, we are offered the gift of quieting the noise of our daily patterns and the possibility of hearing God a little more clearly. I have learned that for me, and for many of the people of God in the past, the wilderness—away from the normal and the settled sense of the ordinary—is the place where God speaks and leads.

Wilderness as Holy Space

Several times in Scripture, we are told that God is holy and that we, as God's people, are to be holy. But what does that mean? Like my early understanding of wilderness, the idea of holiness that I held from my youth was a bit off. I used to think of holiness as some sort of radical goodness, the kind of attribute that causes radiant light to shine and unblemished feet to hover inches over the ground with angelic choirs singing four-part harmonies. That is holy, in one sense.

> As our lives become unsettled and we face situations that jar us from our routines.

The Hebrew word that we translate as "holy" is *kadosh*. At its root, it indicates something like apartness or separateness. To be holy is, in effect, to be other, to be unusual, to be weird or not normal.

God is deeply holy in the sense that God is other, God is unique, there is none like God. In the Psalms, the authors again and again describe the uniqueness of God. I encourage you to read the Psalms and all the praise hymns found throughout Scripture and substitute "unusual" or "strange" for "holy." The experience is, in a word, *weird*. As it should be! When the word of God becomes something other than comfortable and ordinary, we know that we are on the road to someplace interesting and possibly holy.

When we take a road to a literal or metaphorical place that is other than our ordinary, civilized experience, it is possible, and even likely, that we will encounter the holy. As our lives become unsettled and we face situations that jar us from our routines—and dare I say, complacency—we are forced into a wilderness encounter with the holy/strange/other. It is my hope that in reading my words, and then prayerfully considering your place in the world, you will have a holy encounter with God. That is, I wish for you the uncomfortable and abiding strangeness of wilderness.

A Bit about My Thinking Partners

When I read books on theology especially, but really any topic, I like to know, as best I can, where the author is coming from. Who are their influences? What do they care about? What caused them to think like they do? I want to be sure to do for you what I always wished would be done for me, albeit briefly. I lived in literal wilderness places in eastern Morocco and southern Israel for most of my adult life. God spoke to me powerfully there. But God has also spoken to me when I feel lost, confused, and disoriented in suburban Indiana, where I now live. I am passionate about helping others think through their own wilderness experiences.

As I did my master's in Arabic and Hebrew, my PhD in Jewish studies, and now my MDiv, I relied heavily on three intellectual traditions that you will see throughout the rest of this book. The first tradition is early rabbinics. In times when I have been assailed by questions and uncertainty, I have found comfort in the conversations and questions raised by the rabbis as they struggled with their own wilderness experiences. After the second temple was destroyed by the Romans around 70 CE, after the transformation of Christianity from a Jewish cult to a catholic religion, and after the dispersion of Jewish life all over the globe, the rabbis struggled with how to understand ancient Holy Scriptures in new, relevant ways and how to preserve traditions without letting them become ossified and irrelevant. I think their approaches and some of their solutions are valuable for us today as we also struggle to make sense of our traditions and adapt them for the future.

The canonical approach of Brevard Childs and the rhetorical criticism of Phyllis Trible,[3] among others, are the second major influence in my scholarship. They view the biblical text as we have it as the base unit of analysis and insist that we interpret Scripture as a whole. Despite having a PhD in a subset of a Hebrew Bible program, I have never been interested in a source-critical approach to Scripture. In many cases, tearing apart Scripture limits life-giving interpretive possibilities and uproots sections of the Bible from surrounding passages that are essential for interpretation. For instance, seeing Genesis 1 and 2 as two separate accounts woven together somewhat ham-fistedly is much less romantic and interesting to me than reading about how the first humans were created as both male and female (Gen 1:27)—that is, two-sexed (BT *Ketobut* 8a, Genesis Rabbah 8:1, Gen 5:2). Then only after the initial creation was one of the humans split into two separate male *or* female individuals. If Adam and Eve emerged from the garden to find many other two-sexed humans, suddenly questions about who Cain was afraid of (Gen 4:14) and who Cain and his descendants (and Seth and his descendants) married

(4:17) provide fertile scriptural grounds for imaginative answers that are consistent with internal biblical narratives. This is just one example of how keeping the canon together leads to more interpretive possibilities and, quite frankly, more fun. Accordingly, I will not talk about how the Bible was cobbled together or redacted, but I will discuss how one section of Scripture helps us understand or troubles another section. This approach can lead, and has led, to critiques of me and others in this tradition as reading Scripture uncritically. This is a fair accusation, to a point. But not critiquing sources is not the same as not critiquing the text. In my own journey with Scripture, I find that my wrestling with the text, and the Holy Spirit wrestling with me through the text, is much more fruitful when I have to wrestle with the text as a whole. This is, of course, my experience. Others have found profound blessings and liberatory readings of Scripture through critical approaches.[4]

The last of my major influences has been the collective of the many teaching theologians I have had the pleasure of studying under, working with, or simply struggling and growing with by studying their work. That the majority of these theologians have been women has been important to me in undermining and correcting an androcentric view of Scripture and the world. Kathryn Schifferdecker, Fleming Routledge, Marg Mowczko, Amy Lindeman Allen, Carol Newsom, Danya Ruttenberg, Amy Marga, Meesh Hammer-Kossoy, Avivah Gottlieb Zornberg, and the inimitable Rachel Held Evans have made me a better scholar, Christian, and human. I am grateful to live in the same time as them and to share the earth with such women.

Chapter Descriptions

When I set out to organize this book about living life in the wilderness, it occurred to me that there is already a book of the Bible whose main characters have dealt with this experience. Often overlooked by many readers, the book of Numbers will help provide structure for the following chapters. The Hebrew title of the book, *Bmidbar*, simply means "in the wilderness." It is a fitting title for the work that catalogs the experience of the Israelites after leaving slavery in Egypt and receiving the Law from God at Sinai—before entering and settling the promised land. This wilderness time was an in-between place where God and God's people were figuring out how to interact with each other. Discovering how this relationship was going to work was a spiritual, relational, political, and geographic wilderness. Although *Bmidbar* is frequently glossed over, I feel it has much to teach us Christians about the life of faith in between the already accomplished salvific work of Jesus and the full realization of God's coming kingdom. Accordingly, I will use some of the basic themes of Numbers to guide this work.

The first chapter will focus on who God is to us as we journey through the wilderness. I will use Numbers chapters 1–10 as a springboard to discuss the importance of knowing and believing who God is as revealed both historically and in our own lives. This step is foundational and will serve the same purpose as orienting sandals in the night so that even when the sandstorms of life blow and seek to disorient us, we will retain our orientation as we seek to be closer to the author and protector of our faith.

The second chapter focuses on the wilderness as a place of tempting and testing where we face ourselves to determine who we really are. When we are unmoored from the ordinary and habitual, decisions that were instinctual and barely conscious become a source of confusion, and each action has to be intentional. I will consider the examples of temptation and trials that the Israelites faced in their desert wanderings as a prototype for the temptations that both Jesus and we face in wilderness places.

The third chapter considers the wilderness itself as a place where we encounter, hear, and even see God. The Bible, in both the Old and New Testaments, is replete with instances of patriarchs, prophets, kings, and the Messiah seeking out wildernesses as places where they can speak with and listen to God. More than at any other time in Israelite history, however, the book of Numbers describes a period when the entire nation was able to clearly and indisputably see for themselves what God wanted them to do as a people.

The fourth chapter considers the examples of women in the wilderness. In times of confusion and disorientation, women have stepped forward and led the way toward righteousness and justice. Numbers recounts a few of their stories and provides fodder for how we might witness women doing the same today.

The last chapter will focus on the wilderness as a place where it is possible to shrug off the ordinary and move forward into holy weirdness. Even after repeated sin and falling short of God's hopes for them, the Israelite community was able to use the deaths of their former leaders to start over as God called a new generation and new leadership to pursue what God had promised and desired for them. In the same way, wilderness experiences offer believers a place to reorient, to take stock of what has become the normal pattern of life, and to consciously decide what to maintain and what to abandon as they move forward into intentional life.

Each chapter will conclude with a series of questions meant to guide reflection and conversation with others. Whether you engage with the questions or not, my desire is that you will be blessed by this book to contemplate God's role in your life, especially in the wilderness places.

To that end, I hope these chapters will guide you through a journey that the Lord has blessed me to take repeatedly, from the city to the wilderness and back. In following this cycle, we imitate Jesus, who "often withdrew to lonely places and prayed" (Luke 5:16 NIV) before coming back to the cities and crowds. If our Messiah found value in seeking God in the wilderness but did not abandon the cities and people, perhaps that pattern will be useful for his followers too. It has been for me.

GUIDED REFLECTIONS

1. Think of times when you have been lost, confused, or disoriented, either in geographic space or in your life more generally. How do you remember those times? Were they intense, fruitful, horrible, or something else? Why?

2. How does the idea that *holy* means something like "weird" in the biblical text trouble your notions of

God as holy? How does it make you think about holy/ weird people, places, and ideas differently?

3. What intentional wilderness space, either geographic or in your life, could you or do you desire to seek out?

1

Preparing for the Journey:
Who Is God?

The Lord appeared to him from far away.
I have loved you with an everlasting love;
    therefore I have continued my faithfulness to you.
                                   —Jeremiah 31:3

Because you are precious in my sight,
    and honored, and I love you,
I give people in return for you,
    nations in exchange for your life.
                                   —Isaiah 43:4

In this chapter, we will remind ourselves (because reminding and remembering are central to the life of faith) what most folks who have had a relationship with God already know on some level: interacting with God is complicated and messy. God is concerned not just with loving God's children but also with preserving God's holiness. God's intimacy with us is always caught up in God's world-creating majesty. God's power and proximity are often revealed most directly in the wilderness. Scripture provides models, such as the prophets and the Messiah, who demonstrate intimacy with God by asking God to assert God's power at the same time that they experience intense emotional bonds with humanity. And lastly, we will consider how the biblical text openly describes God's emotional experiences in the wilderness places of God's relationship with people.

Walking the Wilderness

While living on the edge of the Sahara, when I knew I would be going for a long wilderness walk the next day, I had to prepare the night before. At least twelve hours before I would exit the town, village, or small farm, I would start drinking copious amounts of water and add a bit of salt to whatever food I was eating to make sure the water stuck with me. Then I would rise early in the morning in order to do as much walking as possible before the hottest parts of the day. Before I set out, I made sure that I had a little bit of money, but not so much that I would worry about losing it. And especially in rural Morocco, I carried my trusty sling and four or five stones to protect against packs of feral dogs.

The comparisons to David slinging rocks to protect himself and his sheep are, I suppose, inevitable at this point, but I should note that I am a terrible shot. Rather than relying on accuracy to hit any of the dogs, I selected flat stones that in a different context would be excellent for skipping over the surface of calm water.

These stones, when flung out of a sling at high velocity, emit a ferocious buzzing sound as they slice through the air. The sound alone of a rock hurled in the right direction was sufficient to scare off the alpha dog and then, accordingly, the entire pack, even if my aim was never close to true (which it was not). Generally, I find it better to be noisy than cause real injury anyway.

Beyond what I would bring, I prepared my route in order to take advantage of the hospitality of friends and any natural sources of water along the way. And even more important than visiting places that would meet my physical needs (because I never spent more than a few days in the wilderness at a time), I had to prepare for my mental needs. Walking around without other humans for miles and miles can be a comfort for some, and especially in a setting that is a lush, verdant forest with plenty of resources. But crossing a hot, arid high desert for days at a time requires as much mental preparation as it does physical, if not more.

A wandering mind can miss the small signs of a water source or a group of predators. A sense of loneliness or homesickness can be a fleeting dark spot on a day in the city that is otherwise filled with distractions and the possibility of interesting interactions. But as I journeyed, I was alone with my thoughts and the sound of my breathing and footfalls, sometimes for over one hundred hours at a time. This wilderness time allowed me plenty of opportunities

> But crossing a hot, arid high desert for days at a time requires as much mental preparation as it does physical.

to process my parents' divorce happening on another continent, to ponder why I was never able to make it work with the woman I thought I loved in college (and thank goodness, because we are both happily married to other people now!), and to think through my hopes and plans for the future. But it also allowed for hours and hours of self-doubt and regret about situations I would never be able to change. It was a space that seemed to invite the dark stranglehold of depression and anxiety that I have struggled with over the years to assert itself.

In order to avoid these dangers and capitalize on these opportunities, I found it was useful to prepare in advance. I would set out a thought agenda filled with mental tasks that I wanted to accomplish and the emotional work and pondering that I needed to do. Even more importantly, I would ask God to bring to mind what I should pray about as I walked several hours the next day. I have never been excellent at focusing on any task for more than a few minutes (without the aid of a good book, that is). Having a to-do list of tasks that I could accomplish in my head and heart while walking to the far villages helped me focus on the task at hand. The time and space also allowed me to do some heavy mental and emotional lifting. Those wilderness walks have always been a particularly important time in my relationship with God as well. More on that later in this chapter.

The key for me in having a successful journey in the wilderness was always to prepare ahead of time for whom and what I would meet on the journey. We can never foresee all of the outcomes we will face as we journey through the wilderness, but successful preparation will help mitigate the potential for disaster and prepare for the best possible interactions. This principle is clear from the first few chapters of the book of Numbers.

Who Is God in Numbers?

Various biblical scholars break down the book of Numbers in different ways, but there is generally some agreement that the first section of the book, from 1:1 to 10:10, constitutes a unit and centers on preparing and organizing the Israelites for a military march through the hostile wilderness, with God in their midst. To that end, the Israelites were counted and sorted multiple times and told where to camp, how to march, and what to do with God's dwelling in the camp. God's presence is a source of *hope* and *danger* for the Israelites as they march.

For Christians who are accustomed to having God's Holy Spirit living within them and a risen Savior interceding with God the Father on their behalf, the sheer weirdness of having *a* god, much less *the* God, living among humans can be difficult to comprehend. For the Israelites, who saw God's wonders performed among them while they were still in Egypt and who then heard the voice of God at Sinai, the presence of God was profoundly real and shaped their reality. Avivah Gottlieb Zornberg says, "Here, the generation of the wilderness emerges as the generation of extraordinary spiritual experience, receivers of the Torah to the fullest extent, fed on miracles and nurtured directly by God: a generation of ecstatic faith. They are known as *dor de'ah*—a generation of *special knowledge*."[1]

Occasionally, I feel the gentle nudging of the Spirit, and I pray to have God reveal God's will to me. Sometimes I feel like

God grants that prayer. But imagine, if you can, seeing the sky turn black but still being able to see (Exod 10:21–23) or walking through a body of water on dry ground (Exod 14:21–22; and the text repeatedly insists that the ground was dry, not swampy or wet sand). Imagine further that you—and your whole family and everyone you know—hear the very *voice* of God at the same time at the base of God's mountain (Deut 4:9–13; 4:32–36; 5:1–4). The Israelites' experience of God was overwhelming, even as God inhabited the top of the mountain while the people were at the distant base camp. But God wanted to be even closer.

As the people prepared to march together to the promised land, God announced that God would dwell in the worship center right in the very center of camp;[2] God would be present in the midst of God's people! The question of how the Lord of the universe can dwell in a specific place has long frustrated theologians, but Trinitarian Christians should not be bothered by the thought of God being physically manifest in one particular place and time. The presence of God living among God's people calls to mind for Christians the presence of Jesus among his disciples. It should also cause us to recall the intimacy of Adam and Eve in the garden before the expulsion. God used to take strolls in the cool of the evening looking for the humans, presumably to have an afternoon walk and talk. But just as sin in the garden made continued intimacy with God impossible, so the Israelite community struggled with faithfulness even with the holy God dwelling in their midst. God does not set people up for failure, however. The first ten chapters of Numbers set out a system whereby this new phenomenon in the world—a postfall situation of God living among God's people[3]—could successfully occur. Maintaining the ongoing close proximity between God and God's people was based chiefly on the people (1) respecting God's holiness and (2) remaining aware of God's intimacy.

In order to help with the first requirement of remembering and respecting God's holiness, God placed the Levites as a physical barrier between God's tent (the tabernacle) and the tents of the rest of the Israelites. God established a sort of uninhabited wilderness right in the middle of the camp to ensure that the Israelites did not traipse through that space as if it were just the same as their common living space. This unsettled space was a true wilderness, but at the same time, it was a space where God chose to concentrate God's presence. In order to ensure the proper holiness/weirdness of God's dwelling, God instructed Moses, "When the tabernacle is to

> God established a sort of uninhabited wilderness right in the middle of the camp.

set out, the Levites shall take it down; and when the tabernacle is to be pitched, the Levites shall set it up. And any outsider who comes near shall be put to death. The other Israelites shall camp in their respective regimental camps, by companies; but the Levites shall camp around the tabernacle of the covenant, that there may be no wrath on the congregation of the Israelites; and the Levites shall perform the guard duty of the tabernacle of the covenant" (Num 1:51–53).

The Levites had a twin task: (1) to make sure that no unauthorized Israelite broke through to step into God's holy place and

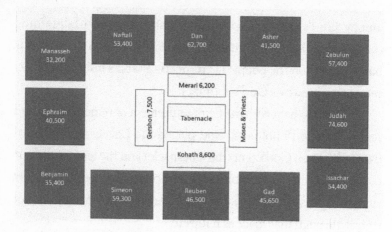

Figure 1.1 The Israelite camp with tribes on the outside, the Levites in between, and God's tent at the center (see Num 1:50–2:31)

(2) to make sure that God's wrath did not break out against the Israelites when they sinned. In both cases the Levites acted to insulate the people from God's holiness and ensured. a space that was not normal in the inner cordon around God's tent.

Even those who had business in the camp needed to be properly cautious. Aaron's sons Nadab and Abihu committed some sort of violation in their roles as priests when they offered an unauthorized fire before the Lord and were thus killed (Lev 10 and Num 3:3–4). They had undermined the holiness of God's dwelling and brought a "strange" fire (that is to say, from God's perspective, in which "holy" is the regular situation). They brought a "common" or "normal" ember or torch from Israelite domestic cooking fires to a place where absolutely everything should be special/weird/ holy and devoted solely to the Lord.

Likewise, the Kohathites, who were in charge of carrying the most holy things when the Israelite camp moved (Num 3:31), still had to be careful when they entered the tabernacle so that they did not see or touch any uncovered objects of holiness that were above their pay grade: "Then the Lord spoke to Moses and Aaron, saying: You must not let the tribe of the clans of the Kohathites be destroyed from among the Levites. This is how you must deal with them in order that they may live and not die when they come near to the most holy things: Aaron and his sons shall go in and assign each to a particular task or burden. But the Kohathites must not go in to look on the holy things even for a moment; otherwise they will die" (Num 4:17–20).

As generally happens when humans are told not to do something, several Kohathites eventually took umbrage that they were only allowed to carry the holy things rather than being able to participate in the ministerial tasks assigned to Aaron and his sons. As we see in the text above, however, God was greatly concerned for the lives of the Kohathites and warned Moses about the special care that needed to be taken so that they would not transgress the levels of holiness that they were allowed to approach.

Clearly, God was deeply serious about the treatment of God's space at the center of the camp. This is not to say that God, like a bad roommate, wants to live among people but never interact with them. On the contrary, the point of the tabernacle was that God wanted to live among God's people and offer a legitimate meeting place for those seeking to repent and offer gifts respectfully while fully acknowledging God's holiness.

The other overwhelming aspect of God's presence in the camp, besides God's holiness, was God's intimacy. God points out through the book of Numbers that for their own safety, people need to remember that God lives in the camp among the people (Num 5:3) and to act accordingly. God's continuing presence would have been a difficult feature to forget, because the central symbol of God's presence, whether the Israelites were camping or moving, was immediately visible to all of them every morning:

> On the day the tabernacle was set up, the cloud covered the tabernacle, the tent of the covenant; and from evening until morning it was over the tabernacle, having the appearance of fire. It was always so: the cloud covered it by day and the appearance of fire by night. Whenever the cloud lifted from over the tent, then the Israelites would set out; and in the place where the cloud settled down, there the Israelites would camp. At the command of the Lord the Israelites would set out, and at the command of the Lord they would camp. As long as the cloud rested over the tabernacle, they would remain in camp. (Num 9:15–18)

The visible presence of the Lord in the fire and cloud was immediately visible to all the Israelites. If ever they doubted that God was with them in the wilderness they were traversing, they only had to look over to God's tent to behold God's presence.

Even in the midst of anger and punishment, God proved to be especially visible. After the Israelites complained about the report of the spies sent into the promised land, as God was about to call for punishment, the Bible says, "Then the glory of the Lord appeared at the tent of meeting to all the Israelites" (Num 14:10b). Likewise, during the Kohathite rebellion, "the glory of the Lord appeared to the whole congregation" (Num 16:19b). Even when the people complained about the situation into which God had brought them, God's instinct was not to hide or go away; God was revealed even more fully to the entire community.

Encountering God in Our Own Wilderness Places

These Israelite encounters with God in the wilderness should be instructive for an encounter with God today in whatever wilderness we find ourselves. The first point to remember is that God is along for the journey. God did not free the Israelites from Egypt and then say, "Hope it goes well; write when you have work," but God journeyed with them to Sinai and gave them God's righteous and perfect law (Deut 4:4 and Ps 19:7). Even then, God did not say, "Keep the law or get smitten! Now on your way!" God continued on with them and lived among them in the midst of the wilderness camp.

At modern Passover Seder meals celebrated by Jewish folks, one of my favorite parts is singing "Dayenu." It is a song that describes God's acts of redemption, each followed by the assembled singing a chorus that translates to "[It would have been] enough for us." The meaning is clear: wherever and in whatever situation God has carried us, it would have been a blessing because the Holy One would have intervened in history on our behalf. God *keeps* intervening and continually blessing the Israelites from slavery to freedom, by giving the law, by providing for their needs in the desert, by helping them overcome the forces arrayed against them, and finally by bringing them into the promised land. This gracious continuity of miracles proves God's ongoing love. As Christians who have been grafted into this beloved community of God's people, we believe and trust that God's ongoing love is for us as well.

This great love is not something that should be taken for granted, however. God is holy. If it helps to think of it this way, God is *weird*. In fact, it is dangerous to forget that God is holy and powerfully "other." God is not just an other in the sense that each of us humans is other. God is altogether different from us, to the point of challenging and undermining our sense of normalcy. I hope to recover some of that holy strangeness for God. Treating God with complacency and irreverence can still negatively influence our relationship with the Creator of the universe. We miss a key aspect of God's character when we approach without due respect for the otherness of God.

> This gracious continuity of miracles proves God's ongoing love.

But lest we let the pendulum swing too far toward acknowledging God's separateness, let us remember finally that God accompanies *intimately*. God dwelt in the camp, in the midst of God's people. God sought to be heard and, on a few occasions, show God's glory. It is right to worship and respect God for God's sovereignty and power. But if that is the totality of our relationship with God, we miss the key movement: God wants to be with us, among us, around us.

Accordingly, we do not seek to partition our lives, presenting some parts to God and hiding others. Rather, the goal, especially during the wilderness times in which we abandon the familiar and the ordinary, is to present our whole selves to a holy God who demands respect but desires to be our neighbor. This is who God presents Godself to be to the Israelites in their wilderness. Preparing God's people for God's presence was the crucial first step in preparing for the wilderness journey. How does God prepare us to experience God's presence today?

Who Is God *to Me*?

After listening to a series of sermons on MP3 CD (back in the day), I was inspired to ask the question, "Who is God to me?" During twenty-four years of prior church attendance, I had never thought to ask such a personal question. So much of Sunday school and religious education/formation involved answering the questions "Who do the creeds say that God is?" and "Who does Martin Luther / John Wesley / Saint Augustine say that God is?" Growing increasingly dissatisfied with this line of questioning, in my late teens I started to ask, "What does the Bible say about God?" I ruthlessly tossed aside the wisdom of the creeds and religious leaders with the hubris and certainty that only teenagers possess. I still have not entirely recovered from this process, much to the chagrin of my professional Christian friends and colleagues (I mean "professional" in the sense of people who are paid, such as pastors, seminary professors, and the like). In the midst of this *ad fontes* process of jettisoning the human decisions of councils and saints to return to the biblical text for information about who God is, I would never have thought to ask such a question as, Who is God *to me?*

At first, the question seemed so irrelevant. Who cares who God is to me? The Ruler of the universe could not possibly be defined, limited, or understood in relation to me—only to Godself, right? As I began to study more, and as I repeatedly listened to an audio Bible during long desert walks, it became clear that thinking through who God is to communities and individuals is a central concern of the Bible itself. Most of this testimony of who God is comes in the form of names. The name Adam means "human," Eve means something like "living," Abraham means something like "father of the nation," and Sarah means something like "princess." These names each describe an individual person in the ongoing story of God's people.

Beginning with Abraham's servant Eliezer, something interesting happens. Names begin to describe something about God rather than the person. Eliezer means "my God is [my] help." Isaac means "he laughs." In the story of Isaac's naming, Sarah (who is a woman, obviously) laughs when she is told that she will bear a son in her old age. It is God who has the last laugh in the situation, and the child is named Isaac/*Yitzhak* (probably in the original form, *Yitzhak El*, meaning "God laughs"). Isaac's half-brother Ishmael is named thus because "God hears" Hagar's prayers. Jacob is renamed *Israel*, "God wrestler," which takes for granted the physical intimacy God is prepared to embrace in order to steer God's children.

The tradition of names proclaiming/prophesying something about who God is to humans is not limited to the patriarchs. The name *Gabriel* proclaims, "God is my hero!" Michael's name asks the rhetorical question, "Who is like God?" Moses, an Egyptian name, still points to the saving work of God. Ramses's name announces that "Ra [an ancient Egyptian god of the sun] draws out." Moses, whose being drawn out of the river Nile owed more to the true God than Ra, jettisoned the first part of his Egyptian name and simply became Moses, or possibly *Yahmoses*, "the Lord draws out." Daniel's name announces that "God is my judge." Ezekiel's name boasts "God is my strength." Jeremiah's name declares "the Lord is exalted." Hezekiah's name asserts that "the Lord is my strength." The name Immanuel (Isa 7:14) is translated as "God is with us." Isaiah's name means "the Lord is salvation." Several hundred years later, Jesus the Messiah was given another form of Isaiah's name, *Yehoshua*, which also meant "the Lord saves." Names throughout the biblical text have testified to who God is to the name-bearer, his or her parents, or the entire people of God.

I'm told that my name, Cory, means something like "helmet" in Gaelic. It is a fine name, especially for those born in the 1980s in the United States. Throughout my life, I have received several head wounds and injuries (mostly from my older brother) and I am not dead yet, so there may be something prophetic about the name for me. But in Morocco, Cory means something like a septic pit where animal waste is stored until it can be used as fertilizer. Because I longed for a better name than "poop puddle" (as one English-speaking Moroccan friend called me) and I had spent a long time contemplating naming conventions in the Bible that claim something about who God is to people, I spent one of my wilderness walks praying and thinking about a name reflecting who God is to me.

I needed the relational claim of God specifically and purposefully interacting with me. I had lived in Morocco for several months and had survived a tough winter in the high desert. I had no heater in my home, and because the buildings were made out of brick and cement, the outside temperature was warmer than the inside temperature except when the wind was howling. More than my physical situation, my own sense of loneliness chilled my heart. I had left family and friends to come overseas. I am not an outgoing person by any means, and it would be another several months until I really made new friends. The internet had not made its way out to rural Morocco with much reliability in those days. I felt desperately alone. The long walks out to the villages were frequently my only distraction from my growing depression.

> I spent one of my wilderness walks praying and thinking about a name reflecting who God is to me.

When I went on my prayerful walk, I started early and covered about ten miles out into the desert along one of my favorite routes that led to a river valley that went deep into the High Atlas mountains. It was the middle of the Sahara summer, and the river was dry on the surface. Farther into the mountains a trickle of water was visible, but most of the water from the snowmelt ran under the ground, trapped above layers of rock that made up the mountains and that the water was not able to penetrate. I walked along, praying, oblivious to the water table and surrounding geology.

I did not want to be annoying to God by asking the same question over and over, but I was stuck wondering, "God, who are you to me?" When I pray, I am frequently guided by two teachings of Jesus. The Messiah, I figure, knows a thing or two about talking with God, and when he instructs his followers on how to pray, we would do well to listen. The first bit of guidance comes from Matthew 6:7–8: "When you are praying, do not heap up empty phrases as the Gentiles do; for they think that they will be heard because of their many words. Do not be like them, for your Father knows what you need before you ask him."

Long prayers in church that seem to go on and on, especially with repeated, formulaic phrases, always make me wonder if we could do with another review of Jesus's instructions here. Yesterday (I'm writing this on a Monday), someone prayed after the sermon for the better part of a half hour, growing more and more agitated until he was yelling into the microphone. I had to take my one-year-old out of the service because he was frightened by the ruckus. Maybe this is a side benefit of my lack of a long attention span, but I have never been at risk of violating Jesus's command not to multiply empty phrases while praying. My mind starts to drift if I pray for much more than a minute or two.

The second instruction of Jesus that I find very valuable is the guidance to pray as one who will not give up (Luke 18:1–9). Jesus said to pray like a widow who threatens an evil judge so much that he grants her justice so that she will not give him a black eye (*hupópiazó*). In Luke 18:5, *hupópiazó* was a technical term in boxing, meaning to hit just under the eye in such a way that the opponent's face sustains colorful bruises.[4] The interpretation of this passage has been frequently scandalizing to me. Jesus seems to liken God to an unjust judge who is *annoyed* into fulfilling the petitioner's request! But the text argues the opposite. Jesus says to listen to what the unjust judge says. If evil humans can be threatened into eventually fulfilling requests by the intimidating persistence of people they do not care about, how much more speedily will God respond to God's chosen ones when they cry out repeatedly (Luke 18:6–8)? This is some real chutzpah for Jesus to describe the ungodly judge as being in the same position as God to grant requests. But then Jesus emphasizes the difference between the evil judge and God using a rabbinic technique called *kal v'chomer* (light and heavy) to say that if persistence works in the relatively minor case of an evil judge and a widow he does not care about, how much more will it work in the case of the good God who presumably desires to vindicate God's elect?[5]

Drawing from these two passages, I tend to prefer to pray short prayers repeatedly, with plenty of breaks to think about something else, rather than struggle through long prayers that ask for the same thing in multiple ways. I am aware that these verses in the Bible support my personal preferences, so I hope I am not simply choosing texts to justify my thinking. Still, I feel pretty comfortable with Jesus's words, and anyway, God answered me.

As I neared the crest of a hill that I had climbed on the way over to the river valley, I asked God once again, "Who are you to me?" for perhaps the twentieth time in the last two hours. It was at that moment that my foot struck a rock. I do not remember kicking it, or it may have just tumbled out from underneath my foot and rolled down the minimountain. It dropped with a ker-plunk into a hole that I had not perceived. Like Moses investigating the strange sight of the burning bush, I walked over to see this strange thing—a hole in the desert that sounded like it had water in it. What I found was not a small puddle but a racing underground stream with clear, cool water! God spoke to me in that moment and said, "I am your water in a dry and thirsty land." This pronouncement—delivered not audibly but with a deep assurance that it was directly from God—brought to mind the words of Isaiah 44:3 and Psalm 63:1. But this was not a mere recitation of the Bible but a pronouncement of what I already knew to be true: during my literal and metaphorical wilderness wanderings, when I was lonely, confused, unsettled, and unsure what was next in life, God remembered me and was my constant supply and refreshment. This cemented my use of the name that I go by in Morocco: *Zakaria* (the Arabic version of the Hebrew name *Zechariah*), which means "the Lord remembers."

I want to be clear: this water in the desert was not miraculous. It was not like the water God provided for Hagar or Samson in the desert. It was there before, and I have visited the spot since and found the water still flowing. Whether it was geological formations that forced water to the surface or even an open section of pipe from a distant hydroelectric dam that crossed through these parts of the hills was utterly beside the point. The physical water was only a conduit for the real miracle: that God loved me enough to answer a question that I, a mere mortal, posed to the Author of life and the Creator of everything. Not only did God speak, but God spoke of our ongoing relationship and reminded me of what God has already been to me. This was a profound gift and my most important gift from God. As miraculous as that felt to me, however, it follows the clear pattern of God being pleased to respond to God's peoples' repeated requests. We need to be ready to journey with this type of God.

The God Who Loves to Bargain

Many years after the miracle, I told a friend who was in seminary at the time the story of God using the rock and stream in the desert to validate our ongoing relationship and to speak to me of who God is to me. My friend laughed and asked how long I'd been in the desert by that point and if I'd seen any "other mirages." I was deeply hurt by his assuming that my most important story was an illusion or a lie.

My friend was not well acquainted with the notion that God would answer such repeated requests. But Scripture is shot through with stories of those who negotiate and even argue with God. We do not normally think of arguing with God as holy behavior, but some of the people in Scripture with whom God had the closest relationship have felt the freest to bring their petitions to God over and over again. Remember the widow in Jesus's parable, to whom the judge initially said no.

Let me begin with the case of Abraham, the paragon of faith who moved his family to a land that God promised to him and nearly sacrificed his son Isaac because that is what he understood to be God's command (Gen 22).[6] Following God's commands is not about blind, unquestioning obedience. Following God does not eliminate dialogue or requests of God. On the contrary, except in the crucial failure to argue for the life of his son, Abraham's relationship with God had been tested and proven frequently enough that Abraham felt confident to try to change God's mind.

After Abraham had settled in the promised land, he was visited by three angels of the Lord who came to announce the birth of a son (Isaac) to Abraham and Sarah. After they ate a meal together and were preparing to leave, the Bible includes this account:

> Then the men set out from there, and they looked toward Sodom; and Abraham went with them to set them on their way. The Lord said, "Shall I hide from Abraham what I am about to do, seeing that Abraham shall become a great and mighty nation, and all the nations of the earth shall be blessed in him? No, for I have chosen him, that he may charge his children and his household after him to keep the way of the Lord by doing righteousness and justice; so that the Lord may bring about for Abraham what he has promised him." (Gen 18:16–19)

God told Abraham that God was going to investigate reports of wickedness in the cities of the plain. If the reports were true, God would destroy them. Abraham interjected that it would not be very becoming of God to destroy a city with fifty innocent people in it. God agreed that the city would not be destroyed for fifty people. Abraham decreased the number of innocent people needed to save the cities to forty-five, forty, thirty, twenty, and finally ten people. God agreed each time (see Gen 18:20–33).

Immediately, you might think this bargaining with God stuff sounds dangerous. Even Abraham asked God / God's representatives not to be annoyed. But Abraham did not stop asking God for the safety of his nephew, Lot. More importantly, God continued to grant Abraham's request until he stopped asking.

Shockingly, in this bit of Scripture, we are granted a rare glimpse of God's internal monologue. God ponders, "Should I keep a secret from Abraham? No, because I chose him and because he will teach his children *the way of the Lord* by doing righteousness and justice" (paraphrasing Gen 18:17–19). The way of the Lord in this case involves God purposefully revealing God's plans to a chosen servant. But God intended much more than just a conversation, which we see from a close examination of the biblical text. At the end of their conversation, the Lord left when *God* had finished speaking *with Abraham*. God was not finished with the conversation until Abraham was done bargaining! God intended for Abraham to intercede on behalf of the people of Sodom and Gomorrah, or at least on account of his nephew's family. In so doing, Abraham learned the way of the Lord for righteousness and justice: God does not wish to punish the innocent with the guilty, and God's chosen servants will always seek to defend the innocent, even if it is God who attacks.

Abraham thought that ten righteous persons would be enough to save the city because Lot, his wife, and their daughters, sons-in-law, and grandchildren combined were more than ten people (Gen 19:12–15). However, at least two of Lot's daughters chose to side with their in-laws and the murderously inhospitable townspeople, proving themselves to be unrighteous. Lacking the crucial ten righteous people, the cities were destroyed. Even Lot's wife and his daughters who escaped with Lot from Sodom proved to be rather disappointing. Lot's wife disobeyed the command of the angels not to look back at the destruction of Sodom, and Lot's daughters later connived to get their father drunk so he would impregnate them. Despite the destruction of the cities of the plain and the decimation of Lot's family, God agreed with Abraham's continued prayerful bargaining to protect the innocent and granted him his request.

Abraham bargained to save the people of Sodom and Gomorrah. But in streams of rabbinic thought, rather than passing God's "test" (Gen 22:1) by nearly sacrificing his son, he failed it miserably by not bargaining with God for his son's life as he had bargained for the lives of strangers. Relating Jeremiah 7:31 (where God affirms that not only does God not command child sacrifice but it never even occurred to God to require it) to Genesis 22, the rabbis, most noticeably in Bereshit Rabbah 56:8 and then in Rashi's interpretation of Genesis 22:12, hold that Abraham made a colossal error in understanding who God was to him. God asked Abraham to "bring up" his son, not "slaughter" his son. Abraham imagined his God was no different than other gods, so when polyvalent verb possibilities were before him, Abraham understood "offer up" instead of "bring up."

In this reading, God could not help but be impressed with Abraham's devotion and readiness to offer his own son. But God was nonetheless doubly horrified that (1) Abraham was ready to kill his son, whom God had miraculously gifted to him and (2) Abraham understood God to lust after children's blood.[7] In both Judaism and Christianity, Abraham remains the model for faithful obedience and following God's commands, even when those commands could lead to a terrible place. But it is telling that in the biblical account, God never directly speaks to Abraham again after he almost sacrificed his son. This is a stark change from Abraham's earlier frequent conversations with God. Abraham also never spoke with Isaac again, and the rabbis say that upon hearing what Abraham had almost done to her son, Sarah died on the spot from shock and disappointment (*Tanhuma Vayera* 23). Decades later, Jacob would recall God as "the Fear of Isaac" (Gen 31:42, 53) because of the trauma of this moment. Not knowing who God is had drastic generational consequences for Abraham and his family.

For a more successful story of bargaining with God, we turn to Moses. As discussed earlier, after God's appearance (theophany) at Sinai, where the *entire nation of the Israelites* heard God's voice, there was literally nowhere to go but down. And this is exactly what the Israelites did. Even as their leader Moses met with God at the top of the mountain, they chose to ignore God's commands. Instead, they convinced Aaron to create a golden calf that they could see, touch, and offer wild, adulterous worship to. Before Moses even descended from the mountain, he counseled God not to act harshly against the Israelites and thereby spoil God's majesty among the Egyptians. After ascending the mountain again after inflicting punishment himself, he implored God to refrain from collective punishment and to not abandon the Israelites in the desert:

> The Lord said to Moses, "I have seen this people, how stiff-necked they are. Now let me alone, so that my wrath

may burn hot against them and I may consume them; and of you I will make a great nation."

But Moses implored the Lord his God, and said, "O Lord, why does your wrath burn hot against your people, whom you brought out of the land of Egypt with great power and with a mighty hand? Why should the Egyptians say, 'It was with evil intent that he brought them out to kill them in the mountains, and to consume them from the face of the earth'? Turn from your fierce wrath; change your mind and do not bring disaster on your people. Remember Abraham, Isaac, and Israel, your servants, how you swore to them by your own self, saying to them, 'I will multiply your descendants like the stars of heaven, and all this land that I have promised I will give to your descendants, and they shall inherit it forever.'" *And the Lord changed his mind about the disaster that he planned to bring on his people.* (Exod 32:9–14; emphasis added)

Moses's response to God's pronouncement of the people's perfidy is twofold: please do not kill them all, and please forgive and do not abandon us. Before Moses had seen the evil for himself, he told God that if God killed the Israelites and started over with Moses's descendants, the Egyptians would mock God for being evil and intending to kill rather than fully deliver the Israelites. This makes sense, after all, because the Egyptians had just been ravaged by plagues and had driven the Israelites out with all their finery just to be rid of the people whose God was so powerful and dangerous. God saw the wisdom of Moses's argument, agreed with

Moses, *and God changed God's mind*! The Hebrew text actually says that God *felt sorry for the evil he was about to do* (Exod 32:14).

Think about having such an intimate relationship with God that you can offer God advice and God may not only agree with you but repent of God's original plan. This is a God who *loves* to be engaged in conversation with God's beloved children! Twice more in the book of Numbers, God decided to smite the Israel-ites and start over with Moses, and twice more Moses argued with God.

> **God saw the wisdom of Moses's argument, agreed with Moses, and God changed God's mind!**

After the Israelites heard their spies' fearful reports on the giants living in the promised land, they decided to kill Moses and Aaron and find a new leader to take them back to Egypt. God again told Moses that the Isra-elites should be killed and that God would start over with Moses's family. Moses responded, "'Forgive the iniquity of this people according to the greatness of your steadfast love, just as you have pardoned this people, from Egypt even until now.' Then the Lord said, 'I do forgive, just as you have asked'" (Num 14:19–20).

Moses had increased the strength of his argument against God. After reminding God of the intimacy of their wilderness journey so far, Moses argued that the Egyptians would think that God was not merely evil (they probably already did after the death of their firstborns) but also weak! Moses suggested the Egyptians might think that God was so embarrassed at being unable to conquer the Canaanites that God then killed the Israelites all at once in the desert to hide his impotence. Then Moses sang a song in praise of God's steadfast love, forgiveness, and justice. This was sufficient to convince God once again to spare the Israelites.

The incident of the sin of Korah and the Kohathites represents the epitome of hubris and violating God's rules concerning holiness—rules that God enacted specifically to protect the Kohathites, among others. Korah and friends wanted to be priests on the same level as Aaron's descendants. They had a good claim because they were of his clan in the tribe of Levi, but God chose Aaron and his descendants for the highest priestly role. Their frustration is not difficult to understand, really. The Kohathites were allowed to enter the holy of holies to take care of the holiest objects while moving them, but when Israel camped, the Kohathites were not allowed to interact with the sacred objects in the holy of holies. They must have felt so tantalizingly close to full access. Some simply could not stand that others had greater access and more prestige than they did.

So Moses engineered a test to resolve the controversy. He told Korah and all who sought priestly roles to present censers of incense before the tabernacle and see what happened. Korah gathered the entire community to witness what he thought would be his success. God was displeased with Korah's power seeking:

> And the glory of the Lord appeared to the whole congregation.
>
> Then the Lord spoke to Moses and to Aaron, saying: "Separate yourselves from this congregation, so that I may consume them in a moment." They fell on their

faces, and said, "O God, the God of the spirits of all flesh, shall one person sin and you become angry with the whole congregation?"

And the Lord spoke to Moses, saying: "Say to the congregation: Get away from the dwellings of Korah, Dathan, and Abiram." (Num 16:19b–24)

Again, Moses's quick instinct to bargain and plead for mercy saved the larger Israelite community but not the offending families. In the midst of cresting passion and anger, God still welcomed and honored the prayerful attempt to change God's mind.

I want to pause and say very clearly and unequivocally that even though prayerful bargaining worked for Abraham and Moses and has worked for thousands if not millions of others as well, it does not mean that God is bound to grant us everything we request. If that were the case, many beloved saints who have gone to rest and await the resurrection, whose loved ones prayed for healing and restoration, would still be alive, free of pain and disease. Our loved ones suffer not for lack of prayers but because Jesus has not yet returned and the new heaven and new earth have not yet been realized. Prayers of the righteous avail much (Jas 5:16), and God can grant whatever healing and deliverance God wishes. But only with the return of Jesus will suffering and death end.

In the meantime, God is not a cosmic vending machine who will grant what we ask if the right amount of prayers is offered. This kind of thinking negates God's sovereignty and ignores much of the Bible. Abraham and Moses make requests for healing and for the safety of others. This is in line with God's goal for Abraham: that he learns the Lord's ways of righteousness and justice. Therefore, let me be clear that my observation here is that God loves and values the ardently repeated request, not that bargaining with God always works. One more story should suffice to prove the point.

On his last night among the living before he descended to the dead, Jesus chose to celebrate the Passover with his disciples. This was a feast to celebrate how God granted freedom to the Israelites from the forces of evil and domination that manifested through the Egyptian Empire (Exod 12:1–28). Thousands of years after the deliverance of the exodus, the Israelites under Herodian and Roman domination did not feel free. And Jesus, knowing what was to come later that evening, felt even less free. So after the meal was finished, he took the disciples and went to a garden with an olive press just outside the city. Taking his most core group of Peter, James, and John, he went off farther to pray:

> Then he said to them, "I am deeply grieved, even to death; remain here, and stay awake with me." And going a little farther, he threw himself on the ground and prayed, "My Father, if it is possible, let this cup pass from me; yet not what I want but what you want." Then he came to the disciples and found them sleeping; and he said to Peter, "So, could you not stay awake with me one hour? Stay awake and pray that you may not come into the time of trial; the spirit indeed is willing, but the flesh is weak." Again he went away for the second time and prayed, "My

Father, if this cannot pass unless I drink it, your will be done." (Matt 26:38–42)

Jesus, knowing his death was drawing near, pleaded in prayer to God, asking that the cup of suffering be taken away. Thinking about the Son of God spending his last few hours of freedom asking God to change God's mind is somewhat jarring to most Christians. Jesus knew that the salvific work accomplished by his death and then resurrection would be his most powerful act. Further, he was wholly submitted to the will of God, even to the point of resisting commanding legions of angels to free him from the cross (Matt 26:53). When we say the creeds, we skip from Jesus's birth to his death on the cross as if only those two things matter and Jesus was simply born to die. But Jesus lived a life that he did not wish to end by being murdered by the state.

> God listens to those who dare to engage in back-and-forth conversations with the God who loves to bargain.

Instead of stoically accepting this fate, Jesus asked his friends to support him while he begged God to change God's mind about what was to happen the next day. Jesus, the sinless one and our example of holiness, nevertheless concluded each request with the concession that not his will but God's be done. Still, Jesus spent some of his last free moments trying to change God's mind.

This is phenomenally powerful to me and gives me such freedom while praying. Even when I do not know the meaning or importance of a situation (which is almost always), I can have confidence that my Parent in heaven not only is willing to hear my request but delights that I repeatedly ask for guidance and that righteousness and justice be done. No lesser figures than Jesus, Moses, and Abraham demonstrate that in the emotional wilderness of being fearful and concerned for ourselves and others, even when we suspect that God might be behind our difficulty somehow, our holiest action is repeated prayer, even petitioning and bargaining with our God. God takes delight in demonstrating to the beloved community that God is present with those going through difficult places. In fact, God listens to those who dare to engage in back-and-forth conversations with the God who loves to bargain.

I suspect that those who have wrestled with God back and forth in prayer over a matter of great importance, such as illness, death, or loss of a loved one, already know the powerful intimacy that comes from repeated prayerful petition and have experienced God hearing their prayers, even if the request is not fulfilled. In a physical or emotional wilderness, we have only God and ourselves.

After realizing that I have come to the end of my own cleverness, my strength, and my ability to problem solve, I throw myself into begging God for a solution. Frequently, for me, it is this seeking after God for answers and respite that brings my time in the wilderness to an end, at least temporarily. God has met my request or has shown me that God will be intimately present in the difficult wilderness journey ahead. This brings me back to a place that is stable and safe, if not altogether normal. What places has God seen you through as you have pursued God for redress?

The God Who Feels and Acts

God's enjoyment of the exchange with God's people, however, is but one of the many aspects of God's character that at first may feel too familiar or seem too human. As we prepare to enter the wilderness with God, we must be cognizant of the range of God's emotional life as revealed in the Bible. This has caused many poor systematizing theologians to level the charge of anthropomorphizing God against those who delve deeply into God's inner life. This charge is not to be feared, but it should be countered. Humans are made in God's own image, and so similarities between God and the human image bearers are to be expected, not surprising. The goal for the believer, however, should be not to find ways in which God is humanlike but to seek to conform ourselves to the One in whose image we are made.

Nowhere is this argument laid out so elegantly as in the work of Rabbi Abraham Joshua Heschel. In his book *The Prophets*, Heschel argues that the core task of the prophet is twofold: to communicate God's emotional state about an unjust situation to God's people so that they can feel the same anger and compassion that God does and to convince the people of God that they should emulate God's caring, loving, and restorative actions. These two movements—the first of emotional empathy to care about what motivates God and the second a radical reorientation to our fellow human—Heschel calls *theomorphism* and *anthropotropism*, respectively.[8]

We are called to experience the full range of emotions that God experiences. We sometimes think of God as unalloyed love. And while God is love, the God of Scripture has a rich and full emotional life. Indeed, God is a god of feelings/pathos. The biblical text takes great pains to describe the panoply of emotions that God feels:

- Love

  I have loved you with an everlasting love; therefore I have continued my faithfulness to you. (Jer 31:3)

  When Israel was a child, I loved him, and out of Egypt I called my son. (Hos 11:1)

- Compassion

  Indeed the Lord will vindicate his people, have compassion on his servants. (Deut 32:36)

  I led them with cords of human kindness, with bands of love. I was to them like those who lift infants to their cheeks. I bent down to them and fed them. (Hos 11:4)

- Pity

  For the Lord would be moved to pity by their groaning because of those who persecuted and oppressed them. (Judg 2:18)

- Regret/grief

  And the Lord was sorry that he had made humankind on the earth, and it grieved him to his heart. (Gen 6:6)

- Jealousy

  You shall not bow down to them or worship them; for I the Lord your God am a jealous God, punishing children for the iniquity of parents, to the third and the fourth generation of those who reject me. (Exod 20:5)

- Joy/pride

As the bridegroom rejoices over the bride, so shall your God rejoice over you. (Isa 62:5)

I will rejoice in doing good to them, and I will plant them in this land in faithfulness, with all my heart and all my soul. (Jer 32:41)

The Lord, your God, is in your midst, a warrior who gives victory; he will rejoice over you with gladness, he will renew you in his love; he will exult over you with loud singing. (Zeph 3:17)

I have already given several examples of God feeling angry enough to destroy a community. God also frequently feels furious at hypocritical worship by those who neglect the abused and powerless:

I cannot endure solemn assemblies with iniquity.
Your new moons and your appointed festivals
  my soul hates;
they have become a burden to me,
  I am weary of bearing them.
When you stretch out your hands,
  I will hide my eyes from you;
even though you make many prayers,
  I will not listen;

your hands are full of blood.
Wash yourselves; make yourselves clean;
    remove the evil of your doings
    from before my eyes;
cease to do evil,
    learn to do good;
seek justice,
    rescue the oppressed,
defend the orphan,
    plead for the widow. (Isa 1:13b–17)

God experiences emotions intensely. In one verse in an incredibly uncomfortable chapter, Ezekiel expresses God's words as an emotional roller coaster: "So I will satisfy my fury on you, and my jealousy shall turn away from you; I will be calm, and will be angry no longer" (Ezek 16:42). The God of the Bible is not the god of the Greek philosophers who is unmoved, rational, and predictable. God in Scripture is a god of emotional outbursts, of love cresting and anger rising and then dying down.

The prophetic task is to continually reintroduce God's people to God's emotions and to help them feel love for people as well as anger and disappointment toward the neglect of God's holiness and the abuse of God's people. As those who have been created in God's image, we are called to feel similar emotions.

When God was furious at Nineveh and sent Jonah to announce its destruction, the people repented in sackcloth and ashes. They empathized with God's deep anger and disappointment. They were, in turn, spared for identifying with what God felt. The prophet Jonah at first refused to fulfill the prophetic task because doing so would mean empathizing with God's gracious desire to save the people of Nineveh, Israel's sworn enemy. He hated the idea that the people of Nineveh would repent of their wickedness (temporarily) and avoid punishment. And even after his brief sermon turned their hearts, Jonah went off to pout. God wants us to feel the pain of the mistreated and feel disgust for wickedness, just as God does. We can work toward empathizing with God, but by ourselves, this is impossible. Thankfully, God does not expect us to engage in the task alone.

I have been convicted that when I am feeling most lost and confused about what to do, the guiding work of the Holy Spirit conditions our hearts to be sensitive to that which causes God distress and grief and to celebrate and nurture that which is pleasing to God. I have started to feel numb recently, as my ability to feel and empathize is overwhelmed by stories and images of casual inhumanity toward migrants and continued gun violence in the United States. I cannot and should not focus on only what is evil. Poet Jack Gilbert reminds us, "To make injustice the only measure of our attention is to praise the Devil."[9] But at the same time, God wants all of us to feel deeply the pain of our siblings and not avoid it. Such empathy must spur us on toward action.

The prophet Jeremiah complained to God that he was overwhelmed by sorrow to the point that he was no longer able to comfort himself (Jer 8:18). In one of the most heart-wrenching passages of Scripture, the prophet cries out to God, "I am broken over the brokenness of the daughter of my people. I mourn, dismay has taken hold of me" (Jer 8:21 NASB). Jeremiah longs to leave and ignore the people, but knowing that he cannot be rid of his compassion and emotional attachment to the suffering people, he instead wishes that his head was water and his eyes were fountains so that he could weep day and night for the daughter(s) of his people (Jer 9:1–2). God empowered Jeremiah to empathize radically with both God and the people who were reaping the harvest of a systematically corrupt society. The experience was, to put it lightly, overwhelming for Jeremiah. But as much as he would have liked to avoid bearing the weight of such crushing disappointment, sadness, and suffering, it was Jeremiah's task to bear witness to God's emotional life. Jeremiah could not help but also witness to God on behalf of the suffering of the people.

We Christians believe that God makes this ongoing radical empathy with God and humans possible through the redemptive work of Jesus. Transforming our hearts so that we care about what God cares about is simply following the teaching of Paul, allowing ourselves to be conformed to the image of Christ (Rom 8:29), who is the image of God (Col 1:15). After telling his followers to love all people, including their enemies, Jesus commands them to be perfect (from *teleios*, meaning "completely mature / fully formed") as God is perfect (Matt 5:48). Being perfect means loving as God loves and feeling as God feels.

This turning of our hearts toward our neighbors as God does is the anthropotropism that Heschel advocates and the necessary outcome of transformed hearts and caring for the world as God does. Just as a sunflower that follows the movement of the sun across the sky is heliotropic (turning toward the sun), so God is anthropotropic. God could sit back and enjoy life in the heavenly realm, but instead God continually turns toward humans and accompanies us in our wilderness journeys. God is not content to do this alone, however, and calls God's people to also be actively working for the well-being of each other. In every generation of the Bible—and I believe in every generation since—God has been asking a modified version of Cain's question, "Am I my creation's keeper?" and answering in the affirmative. God invites and commands the citizens of the kingdom of heaven to be our siblings' keepers. Central to the law given at Sinai was worship of God and care for God's people. Jesus did not make up the commandment to "love your neighbor as yourself" but merely cited Leviticus 19:18.

To take things one step further, it is not just the "human" emotions that God displays throughout the biblical text that lead to charges of anthropomorphism by well-meaning systematicians but also descriptions of God's body. God sets God's face against evil (Lev 20:6) and also turns God's face toward God's people (Num 6:25). God stretches out God's hand against Egypt (Exod 7:5). God rescues by a mighty arm (Deut 4:34; 5:15). The eyes of the Lord are on the righteous (Ps 34:15) and on the Holy Land (Deut 11:12). God's ears hear prayers (2 Kgs 19:16; Neh 1:6). What are we to make of these words when we know that God is spirit?

Again, we know that we were made in God's image, and as a result of sin, that image has been twisted. I call the things on the ends of my arm that I'm using to type these words "hands." But they are just skin, bones, and muscles. What God defines as "hands" are things that bring an end to oppression and slavery. I look in the mirror and I think I see my "face." God's face is totally turned to act against evil and bless the beloved. In God's reality, a face is what a face does. How I wish to show my true face, my undivided attention, to bless my wife and sons! These things on the sides of my body, I call "arms"; God agrees that they are truly and fully arms when they are used to bring the oppressed out of bondage and slavery and into freedom. It is only in doing the work set out for us that we truly realize what our body is. True, God does not have a body in the same sense that we do. But something of Jesus's work and the reconciliation of all things will enable us, in the resurrection, to have a body that is much closer to the image in which we were first made. Jesus's resurrected body is the firstfruits of our resurrected hope that one day we have holy faces, arms, hands, eyes, and ears.

> What God defines as "hands" are things that bring an end to oppression and slavery.

As an example, the particular Lutheran flavor of Christianity that I am a part of celebrates "God's work, our hands," or doing the practical actions that announce and celebrate God's reign in this world. I have loved this language because I think it is spot on, though perhaps not in the way that the designer of the initiative intended. One of my colleagues does not have a left hand or arm below the elbow. Without denying or seeking to minimize her disability, the work that she does for God's kingdom, specifically on behalf of refugees and immigrants, is the true work of Godly hands, even when not performed by human hand(s).

The goal of allowing God to transform our hearts and use our bodies is to prepare ourselves for a confusing journey. When we find ourselves in different and unfamiliar situations in our lives and all else seems to be disorienting or shifting, we remember that our journey is with God. Guided by the Holy Spirit, we relentlessly remind ourselves that our God, who loves to be engaged and who is passionate about emotional engagement, prepares us and journeys with us every step of the way.

The God that we encounter in the Bible and through earnest prayer is not the God of three-circle charts or even systematic theology. God is complicated and messy. God loves to be intimate with God's people but requires that God's people remember and respect God's holiness. The Lord, I firmly believe, wants to reveal Godself to us in shockingly intimate and personal ways as we journey together in the wilderness. And even more shockingly, the prophets and the Messiah model intimacy with God for us by begging, beseeching, and bargaining with God. God, in turn, loves, enjoys, and honors respectful, desperate, and persistent prayerful engagement. Finally, God—by virtue of revealing Godself through an intimate physical presence with the Israelites in the wilderness, prophetic messages, and eventually the incarnation—seeks to reveal God's emotional life and desire for partnership in working for good in this world.

God has taken monumental steps to reveal Godself to us throughout history, but that is only half the task of improving intimacy. After considering who God is to us, we need to proceed to the question, Who are we?

GUIDED REFLECTIONS

1. As you are or have been in the wilderness or a dark place, how has God made God's presence known to you? How have you suspected God's presence but not been sure?

2. When you think of God's intimacy and holiness in the wilderness camp of Numbers, how do you reflect on a holy God wanting to occupy space among a less-than-holy people? What do you think of God taking steps to make the arrangement work? In what ways may God be seeking to live more intimately with you? Does it feel dangerous or uncomfortable? What work might you do to welcome God's holy intimacy in your life?

3. Who is God to you? How comfortable are you with the idea of God celebrating and marking God's relationship with you?

4. As you read about bargaining with God, does the idea make you feel sacrilegious, more connected with God, or something else? What is something that you could press into in prayer?

5. How can you become more familiar with the God who feels? How can we know God's emotions better? What are some ways that God is calling you into turning toward your sisters and brothers?

2

The Journey:
Who Are We?

See what love the Father has given us, that we should be called
children of God; and that is what we are. The reason the
world does not know us is that it did not know him. Beloved,
we are God's children now; what we will be has not yet been
revealed. What we do know is this: when he is revealed, we
will be like him, for we will see him as he is. And all who
have this hope in him purify themselves, just as he is pure.

—1 John 3:1–3

Up to the last couple years of my life, I have mostly thought of
myself in professional terms. I am a scholar, a writer, and a teacher.
I love to teach Bible, read, travel, and study, but I am not a "kid"
person. But in this season of my life, I am the primary caregiver
of a two-year-old and a six-month-old. I dream of intellectually
fulfilling travel and teaching opportunities. For the moment, however, my days are filled with diapers, babbling, corralling, and

managing little adventures. This certainly is a wilderness time for me. I frequently feel tempted to ignore my kids in order to read, jot down ideas, or listen to a lecture or podcast.

What we do in these times of temptation determines who we are as parents and, indeed, who we are as people. We all claim an identity as a beloved child of God, as in the text from 1 John at the start of this chapter. That is truth! But we are also people with individual personalities. We are known for and identify with certain characteristics. This chapter will be about how God uses the wilderness times in our lives, and the temptations that tend to occur within them, to reveal and confirm who we are.

God longs for relationship with us.

God graciously comes to dwell among God's people in wilderness wanderings, in the incarnated Jesus, and through the Holy Spirit given at Pentecost. In these and in our own experiences we are confronted and frequently overpowered by God's intimacy, holiness, and love. But why does God come to us? I do not think that God is bored or lonely. God longs for relationship with us. My wife's oft-repeated concise summary of the Bible is simply this: God wants to be our God and for us to be God's people. The story of the Israelite's wilderness wanderings is tainted by the well-known examples of the Israelites complaining and being faithless. Even so, hundreds of years after the long trek in the Sinai wilderness, God remembered the time as a honeymoon period when the relationship between God and God's people was being solidified:

The word of the Lord came to me, saying: Go and proclaim in the hearing of Jerusalem, Thus says the Lord:

I remember the devotion of your youth,
    your love as a bride,
how you followed me in the wilderness,
    in a land not sown.
Israel was holy to the Lord,
    the first fruits of his harvest.
All who ate of it were held guilty;
    disaster came upon them,
        says the Lord. (Jer 2:1–3)[1]

Even amid all the failure on the part of the Israelites in the wilderness—and there was plenty—what God recalled later was that they followed God through the wilderness. Yes, they complained and even followed other gods on brief occasions. But they did not quit, and they did not turn around and abandon God, even though several individuals sought to do that very thing. The wilderness is a disorienting place, filled with difficulties. But it is a space through which God led and still leads people in order that they might be tested and choose to follow God. We ask God to lead us not into temptation, or to save us from the time of trial, but God does not always answer those prayers as we would like. God, like any good parent or leader, loves God's people and wants them to grow and develop. To that end, the wilderness is the prime experience through which God takes believers in order to help them grow and mature. Reread that last sentence and know that it is the heart of this book. Jesus tells his followers that they should be perfect as their Father in heaven is perfect (Matt 5:48). As discussed in the previous chapter, "perfect" in that verse could more helpfully be translated as "mature" or "fully developed." Just as our physical bodies benefit from exercise to improve strength and endurance, so overcoming or even merely surviving spiritual challenges results in our being conformed a bit more to the likeness of Christ.

The wilderness is an experience perfectly designed for testing. In the wilderness, we are frequently lonely and unmoored from the normal habits and structures that keep our lives running in the same channel (or rut?). In the wilderness, we must make choices on purpose rather than simply doing as we have always done. Whether we are moving to a new town, finding ourselves after a destabilizing breakup, or experiencing a career shift, a sojourn in the wilderness is, by definition, outside of the normal. It is in this wilderness experience, then, that God gives us the opportunity to sort out who we are and whose we are. Tempting always challenges our identity and reveals our true beliefs. Testing shows us to be faithful followers or shows our need for further maturing. Either way, God's love for us is overwhelming and sufficient. But we are called to faithful maturity, and the wilderness experiences in our lives are opportunities to move in that direction.

Considering the Tests and Temptations in Israel's Wilderness Camp

It will be instructive to consider the sorts of tests and temptations that the people of God went through in order to be forewarned about the tests that we may face in our own wilderness times. So let's start with a consideration of the Israelite camp in the book of Numbers.

On their faces, the following stories seem quite different from our current-day situations, but what the Israelites experienced as temptations in the desert are, at their core, similar to what we face today. What does your wilderness look like? In our individual lives, we may confront clear crises that lead to a wilderness experience that may or may not be shared by even our closest friends. In our communal lives, a time of transition such as a shift in political or church leadership, economic change, or a betrayal or attack can leave us feeling unmoored and as if we are wandering. The Israelites faced all of these issues in the wilderness. We can learn from their temptations and how their responses shaped who they were.

Tempting and Testing at Peor (Numbers 22)

The story of Balaam's difficulty with his donkey is well known to Sunday school veterans. What is not frequently discussed in Sunday schools or from pulpits is where Balaam was going when his donkey turned aside from the killer angel. Balak, king of the Moabites, feared the Israelites' incursion into his land. He partnered with the Midianite leaders to raise funds to hire a diviner named Balaam to curse the Israelites. The goal was to remove God's spiritual protection so that the Israelites could be easily overcome and killed in the wilderness before migrating through Moabite land.

After the beloved but confusing donkey incident of Numbers 22, King Balak induced Balaam to attempt to curse the Israelites three times, but in each episode, Balaam heard from God that he was to bless, not curse, the Israelites. After each subsequent blessing, King Balak took Balaam to another overlook for a different perspective on the Israelites, hoping that perhaps that view might elicit curses instead of blessings. The third attempt took place on the peak of Peor. Immediately after that curse-turned-blessing, the perspective of the Bible returns from focusing on Balaam and King Balak back to the Israelite camp, which had not been, it seems, worthy of blessing:

> While Israel was staying at Shittim, the people began to have sexual relations with the women of Moab. These invited the people to the sacrifices of their gods, and the people ate and bowed down to their gods. Thus Israel yoked itself to the Baal of Peor, and the Lord's anger was kindled against Israel. The Lord said to Moses, "Take all the chiefs of the people, and impale them in the sun before the Lord, in order that the fierce anger of the Lord may turn away from Israel." And Moses said to the judges of Israel, "Each of you shall kill any of your people who have yoked themselves to the Baal of Peor." (Num 25:1–5)

At first, it may seem that this is merely a coincidence, that Balaam attempted to curse from the home territory of the Moabite god that the Israelites adulterously worshipped. But the Bible is very clear that this adulterous worship was planned as a stumbling block to the Israelites: "These women here, on Balaam's advice, made the Israelites act treacherously against the Lord in the affair of Peor, so that the plague came among the congregation of the Lord" (Num 31:16).

Even in the book of Revelation, God recalled Balaam's clever trickery. When he was not able to curse Israel directly, Balaam tried another tactic: "I have a few things against you: you have some there who hold to the teaching of Balaam, who taught Balak to put a stumbling block before the people of Israel, so that they would eat food sacrificed to idols and practice fornication" (Rev 2:14).

Unable to pronounce a curse over Israel, Balaam decided to abandon words and resort to actions. He induced the women of the tribal alliance between the Moabites and Midianites to seduce the Israelites specifically as a means to convince them to worship the god of Peor.

This core story is the foundation for the later Israelite fear and uneasiness around foreign women, such as the depiction of the dangers of Solomon's foreign wives (1 Kgs 11) and the warnings against the returnees from the exile marrying foreigners (Ezra 10 and Neh 13).[2] It is necessary to hew closely to the text in interpreting this passage so that we do not allow misogyny or xenophobia to distort our understanding. Up to this point in Scripture, Judah married a Canaanite and then had children with his foreign daughter-in-law (Gen 38:2, 6). Joseph married an Egyptian daughter of a priest (Gen 41:45, 50). Thus at least three of the twelve tribes of Israel (though probably all of them) were descendants of patriarchs who married and had sexual relations with foreign women. Moses himself had also married a Midianite, maybe even a relative of the women that Balaam and Balak induced to lead Israel into idolatrous worship.

What I am saying is that we cannot read Numbers 25 as a condemnation of exogamy. That misses the point. Instead, we need to read it in light of Numbers 31:16. Balaam and the ruling men of Moab and Midian cynically directed and forced Midianite women to seduce Israelite men into worshiping Baal of Peor as a matter of statecraft. The Moabite and Midianite women are victims in this story of an ancient patriarchy that used their sexuality in an attempt to "trick" (Num 25:16–18) Israelites into forfeiting God's special protection so that the men of Moab and Midian could conquer the Israelites.[3]

That the Israelites were "tricked" is crucial for understanding this passage. Sex with foreigners had been no problem in the biblical narrative so far. The Israelites were only doing as Moses had done—sleep with someone from Midian. But the Israelites were tricked in that this otherwise legitimate sexual union was a means to impel them to worship a foreign god. The Midianite woman Cozbi seems to have played an archetypal role in the deception.

The Semitic root of Cozbi's name means "lie" or "deception."[4] The related Akkadian term meant something like "voluptuous, sexually vigorous."[5] In other words, the Hebrew language of Scripture is not oblique about what this character is doing in the narrative—using sex to deceive or trick.[6] Zimri, the Israelite man who sought to bring Cozbi "to his brothers" (Num 25:6 TLV),[7] may have merely wanted to participate in an orgy, but in so doing, he bypassed the tent of meeting and all those who were mourning for the way that the Israelites had been tricked into idolatrous worship of foreign gods. Where Zimri intended to bring Cozbi to share with others, however, he ended up alone with her in a *qubbah*, or a tent with an unusually high vaulted ceiling. Scholars note that hundreds of years later in the same geographic region, the term was used for mobile tent shrines that housed diviners and the worship of foreign gods, presided over by women priests who were often the daughters of tribal chiefs, exactly like Cozbi.[8] Phinehas burst into not just any tent (the word *qubbah* appears here in Numbers 25 and nowhere else in the Bible) but a purposefully constructed alternative to the Israelite tent of meeting that had been built for the sole purpose of tricking lusty Israelites into worshiping Baal of Peor.

This is the reason that biblical injunctions and warnings about marrying foreign devotees of other gods are coupled with the explanation that it is likely that doing so will turn Israelite hearts away from God. The stories of Rahab and Ruth undermine the notion that marrying foreign women is necessarily wrong or dangerous. Foreigners who did not seek to undermine the worship of God, and especially those who embraced Israel's God, were to be welcomed with open arms. We need to preserve this important nuance that is too often lost, even in feminist commentaries.[9] The events at Peor and the deaths of thousands (Num 25:9) that followed would be indelibly burned into Israelite memory and were meant to serve as a narrowly focused caution against marrying *only* those who would try to seduce people away from worshiping God.

Israelite fornication with Midianite women that led to adulterous worship of a foreign god—while the Israelites' true God defended them from curses—is gallingly offensive. The Israelites, after receiving their freedom from Egypt and miraculous provision during their wilderness journey, succumbed to temptation. God would have been justified in forsaking the Israelite community. But again, God chose to remain with God's people.

The actions of one Israelite seem to have made all the difference in God's continued presence with God's people. While certainly not all Israelites sinned, thousands were punished. As the plague broke out, Moses and the remaining Israelites engaged in tearful repentance en masse before the tabernacle. But the idolatry and adultery were not quite finished. It was here that Cozbi and Zimri appeared:

> Just then one of the Israelites came and brought a Midianite woman into his family, in the sight of Moses and in the sight of the whole congregation of the Israelites, while they were weeping at the entrance of the tent of meeting. When Phinehas son of Eleazar, son of Aaron the priest, saw it, he got up and left the congregation. Taking a spear in his hand, he went after the Israelite man into the tent, and pierced the two of them, the Israelite and the woman, through the belly. So the plague was stopped among the people of Israel. (Num 25:6–9)

As a reward for his zealous violence in preventing further idolatry, Phinehas and his descendants were given the high priesthood. The text even says that Phinehas's violence made atonement for the Israelites (Num 25:13). Just as the Levites secured their position as the holy tribe, set apart for God because of their readiness to do violence for God's zeal (Exod 32:29), Phinehas secured the priesthood for his descendants because of his radical intervention in stopping a particularly recalcitrant and bold expression of succumbing to the temptation of Peor.

Phinehas's violence is and should be troubling. Spearing people who worship differently is horrifying to us today (hopefully). Additionally, because of the polyvalent potential of the Hebrew language, interpreters have pointed out that the description of how Phinehas stabbed Zimri, and especially Cozbi (Num 25:8), can be understood as symbolic retributive rape against Midianites.[10] This horrifying suggestion should be more than enough to dissuade us from idealizing retributive violence. I am not advocating violence on behalf of God. That's not what this is about. I believe Phinehas was commended for not simply weeping and mourning the deception of these sex-crazed Israelites, who were fooled into worshiping other gods by women who, in turn, were forced to use their sexuality as a weapon of a male-directed war. Rather, Phinehas took a stand against the ongoing abuse, deception, and idolatry. I believe, as followers of Jesus, we have to stand against his extrajudicial violence (John 8:7). The takeaway is the need to stand viscerally against the temptation to do evil, especially when that evil involves layers of abuse, deception, and coercion.

We need to be crystal clear that the sin that God is upset about is the worship of a foreign god. The Israelites were allowed to marry people of other nations outside the promised land at this point, and there was no scriptural prohibition on premarital sex, at least for men. If Israelites wanted to have a mass-marriage ceremony with Midianites and then enjoy each other physically, I do not think that would have presented a legal problem. Again, Moses's wife was a Midianite, the daughter of a Midianite priest. But in this case, Balaam cynically used public sex as a tool to induce Israelites into the perverse worship of a foreign god.

As Christians who have received a tightening and intensifying of Mosaic law from Jesus ("But I say to you that everyone who looks at a woman with lust has already committed adultery with her in his heart" [Matt 5:28]), we need to examine all forms of temptation that lead us away from God, including temptation that may be mental or emotional and simply physical or sexual. But we need to also remember that the actual temptations we face may only be a gateway to a truly evil rupture of our relationship with God and our neighbors. For example, pornography is intended to cause lust, but I think it also does something worse: it dehumanizes and debases God's good creation and our neighbors. What do overly sexualized billboards, magazines, television commercials, and pornography on the internet do *after* they promote lust? What I am asking is, To what god is our worship being directed *through* sexual temptation? Are women, particularly, being cynically used by the patriarchy as media products to entice people to worship at the altar of dehumanizing consumerism? I would suggest that it may still be that Baal of Peor receives worship from all over the world.

What are we to do in light of this? I suggest that we could do worse than to follow the spirited zealousness—but *not* the actions—of Phinehas. We should take a public stand against temptation that leads to the idolatrous worship of economic systems and cultures that use human sexuality as a commodity, leading to the dehumanization of ourselves and others. I advocate that this should come from a position of humble introspection and confession.

Jesus helpfully points out that we have plenty of work to do in examining our own lives before confronting others (Matt 7:5). Midianite sex was not the end goal of Balaam and King Balak. Using sex to induce the Israelites to idolatry was. The question, then, is not about what form of temptation faces us but about what giving in to temptation does to our relationship with God and our relationships with our neighbors.

When we are in wilderness times, we can be particularly vulnerable to temptations.

When we are in wilderness times, we can be particularly vulnerable to temptations that can give us a sense of belonging when we are lonely and a sense of control when we feel powerless. For me, it is relatively easy to reject sin that comes from anger, and I find it easy to back down, avoid insulting others, and apologize. But I am an easier target when I feel hurt, especially when it seems like someone important to me has actively chosen against me and in favor of something that seems more important. When my friend chose to catch up on text messages and Twitter while I was sharing about how difficult my job change has been, I was particularly hurt and angry. I did not react well in the moment, and I fell into a tailspin over the next few days, wondering if I was now hopelessly boring and incapable of interesting conversation. For those few days, I stopped trying to connect with other friends and withdrew from my colleagues at work until I got over it. That is a relatively inconsequential example, but I wonder how many opportunities to love my neighbors I may have missed because I chose to concentrate on my own hurt and anger.

In our digital age, distraction is a huge temptation. How can we be on guard and prevent ourselves from getting to a point where we hurt our neighbors? I am never less loving to my children than when they ask for my attention while I am trying to "teach" a colleague or student on Facebook or Twitter. In addition, think about what temptations can ensnare our faith communities: How might the enemy be preventing us all from acting and seeing the fruit of a united, equipped body of Jesus ready to show his love?

In this chapter on testing and tempting, it will be crucial to remember that testing is an opportunity to prove what God hopes to be true about us—that we are God's people! Ultimately, we know that it is God who claims us and that we do not save ourselves. And yet part of the paradox of Christian life is that what we do matters deeply, especially for loving God and our neighbor. All the blessings that Balaam spoke over Israel could have been received and expanded upon had the people been faithful. Instead, twenty-four thousand Israelites died after a gross failure of obedience and fidelity (Num 25:9). In the midst of this failure, however, Phinehas stood out for his radical faithfulness and zeal on God's behalf, and he and his descendants were rewarded accordingly. Phinehas declared who he was—one devoted to the Lord—and as a reward, God intensified that identity of one devoted to Godself by giving Phinehas the high priesthood.

Tempting and testing are opportunities to partner with the work of the Holy Spirit within us. Certainly God, through Jesus, stands ready to save and forgive sins. There remains a call on the followers of Jesus, however, to continue to grow in maturity, love, and self-control. Sadly, God's people have not always displayed such self-control.

The Temptation and Testing of Korah

Before Balak and Balaam appeared to tempt the Israelites, temptation sprang up in their midst from one of their own. A Levite named Korah decided that he was not content with his assigned duties and relative proximity to God's presence in the middle of the camp. He wanted more:

Now Korah son of Izhar son of Kohath son of Levi, along with Dathan and Abiram sons of Eliab, and On son of Peleth—descendants of Reuben—took two hundred fifty Israelite men, leaders of the congregation, chosen from the assembly, well-known men, and they confronted Moses. They assembled against Moses and against Aaron, and said to them, "You have gone too far! All the congregation are holy, every one of them, and the Lord is among them. So why then do you exalt yourselves above the assembly of the Lord?" When Moses heard it, he fell on his face. Then he said to Korah and all his company, "In the morning the Lord will make known who is his, and who is holy, and who will be allowed to approach him; the one whom he will choose he will allow to approach him. Do this: take censers, Korah and all your company, and tomorrow put fire in them, and lay incense on them before the Lord;

and the man whom the Lord chooses shall be the holy one. You Levites have gone too far!" Then Moses said to Korah, "Hear now, you Levites! Is it too little for you that the God of Israel has separated you from the congregation of Israel, to allow you to approach him in order to perform the duties of the Lord's tabernacle, and to stand before the congregation and serve them? He has allowed you to approach him, and all your brother Levites with you; yet you seek the priesthood as well! Therefore you and all your company have gathered together against the Lord. What is Aaron that you rail against him?" (Num 16:1–11)

As Moses pointed out, the families of the Levites had been chosen to be reserved for the Lord in place of all the firstborn Israelites. They had been given a place of honor and responsibility between the rest of the Israelites and God's dwelling. The house of Kohath, of which Korah was a part, had been chosen to carry and guard the most holy articles, including the ark, the tables for showbread, the altars, the menorah, and all the instruments for sacrifice (Num 3:29–31). According to Jewish legend, Korah himself was one of the Levites who had the supreme honor of carrying the ark on his shoulders as the Israelites marched (Numbers Rabbah 18:3). As such, he probably spent more time, at least during marching-intensive days, close to the ark than even Aaron in his role as high priest. Yet still he was jealous and longed for an expanded role.

Let me pause to ask if any of this sounds familiar. How often do we grumble against our leaders, either in church or elsewhere, merely because we want additional prestige and power? To be absolutely clear, I think rallying against abusive leadership wherever it is found is our duty. I firmly believe that not all leaders are appointed by God, contrary to a literalistic reading of Romans 13. The Bible itself, which reports a history of evil kings that God has chosen against, makes this clear. Moreover, God orders prophets to speak against and resist the evil of such kings. Certainly, Jesus and his followers resisted the orders of the governing councils that they not preach the good news (Acts 4:18–19). We see in Scripture that there are times to resist unjust authorities.

That said, unless leaders are acting against Christ, we ought to follow them and support them. Korah did not resist an injustice but sought to elevate himself and his position—cynically using the language of equality to do so. Exalting oneself is frequently the most tempting of sins. Isaiah 14, applied in the context to the king of Babylon, shows the inevitable outcome awaiting those who would seek to elevate their power rather than wait on God to elevate them:

> How you are fallen from heaven,
>> O Day Star, son of Dawn!
> How you are cut down to the ground,
>> you who laid the nations low!
> You said in your heart,
>> "I will ascend to heaven;
> I will raise my throne
>> above the stars of God;
> I will sit on the mount of assembly
>> on the heights of Zaphon;

I will ascend to the tops of the clouds,
  I will make myself like the Most High."
But you are brought down to Sheol,
  to the depths of the Pit.
Those who see you will stare at you,
  and ponder over you:
"Is this the man who made the earth tremble,
  who shook kingdoms,
who made the world like a desert
  and overthrew its cities,
    who would not let his prisoners go home?"
      (Isa 14:12–17).

Korah sought to make himself equal with Moses and Aaron, God's chosen. He sought to elevate himself, as did the king of Babylon in Isaiah 14. But instead, he is remembered for his failed attempt to usurp authority.

Korah was not content to face Moses alone. He spoke deceitfully to the non-Levites who were closest to him: the Reubenites. Remember from the camp diagram that the ancestral house of Kohath, where Korah slept, was located right beside the Reubenites (see figure 1.1).

Korah found sympathetic ears in Dathan, Abiram, and On from that tribe. They supported his rebellion, but they were not so certain of his claim that "all the people are holy" that they would join Korah's gang of plotting Levites and offer censers in front of the tent of meeting. This is the second level of temptation in the story: the temptation to trust upstart leaders instead of those appointed by God.

When first considering this story, I had to ask myself, If I were an ordinary Israelite, how would I know the difference between those who speak for God and others who claim the same? The last section of this chapter is a guided reflection about how we can carefully consider different leadership initiatives. In the case of the Israelites, they had already heard God speaking with Moses on the top of the mountain and had witnessed God's indwelling presence fill the tabernacle after Moses's supervision of construction and dedication. The Israelites had already been fed by water from a rock as well as the miraculous manna and quail. Even if it was unclear whether Korah and his friends should have been allowed to officiate in the tabernacle like Aaron and his sons, it should have been abundantly clear that Moses was God's chosen leader and should be respected when he gave a commandment. That is the opposite, however, of what Dathan and Abiram did: "Moses sent for Dathan and Abiram sons of Eliab; but they said, 'We will not come! Is it too little that you have brought us up out of a land flowing with milk and honey to kill us in the wilderness, that you must also lord it over us? It is clear you have not brought us into a land flowing with milk and honey, or given us an inheritance of fields and vineyards. Would you put out the eyes of these men? We will not come!'" (Num 16:12–14).

Dathan and Abiram could have been forgiven for being deceived by a Levite who, after all, served more intimately with God than the Reubenites. But to deny the work of God through Moses or even through God's direct action in bringing salvation from slavery in Egypt was too far.

It may be useful to step back at this point and consider the nature of community in temptation. The list of those Reubenites who supported Korah's rebellion in Numbers 16:1 included three names: Dathan, Abiram, and On. The list of those who openly rebuked Moses omits On, who is never mentioned again in the biblical text. Spoiler alert: the Reubenites who were swallowed up into the earth, along with *some* of Korah's family (a point we will return to momentarily), were Dathan and Abiram and their families. On escapes both Moses's anger and God's punishment, despite his early participation and support. Why and how? The following relies on extrabiblical sources, so Christians will not find it authoritative, but hopefully it is instructive.

A Jewish legend tells the story of how On's wife saved him and his family (BT Sanhedrin 109b–110a). Upon seeing that her husband had taken a position against Moses, On's unnamed wife tried to reason with him. She told him that if Korah were wrong about his challenge to Moses, he would be challenging God with disastrous consequences. If Korah were correct about his challenge, On's position would not improve. With Moses in charge, On was the student and Moses was the teacher. If Korah were allowed to be equal to Moses—On's wife rightly saw that Korah's rebellion was about acquiring power for himself, not all of Israel—then On would still be the student, but now he would have two teachers rather than one. On responded with Korah's claim that all of Israel is holy, every one of them. On's wife replied that he was correct, that all of Israel was holy and should be modest as well! On's wise wife saved her husband and household.

The number of people who succumbed to temptation and were punished in this example, so far, has been more limited than the previously discussed temptation and folly at Peor. Only 250 would-be priests and a couple of clans of Reubenite supporters had rebelled so far. The rest of the people had presumably seen enough to know that God's favor rested with Moses. However, after the earth swallowed the tents of Dathan, Abiram, and Korah, the next day the Israelites rebelled against Moses, saying, "You have killed the people of the Lord" (Num 16:41). This accusation is at least half-wrong. It was God, not Moses, who killed them. This misattribution caused God to become so furious that a plague broke out. Moses ordered Aaron to bring incense into the midst of the people and make atonement for them. As he did, the plague sent to punish the Israelites stopped (Num 16:41–50).

The last temptation was worse than the first: Korah and his followers supposed themselves to be entitled to more power in the community than they were. They rejected what God called them to do and tried to seize the role that God gave to someone else. The Israelites, however, confused who God and Moses were. Self-aggrandizement is dangerous, but ascribing God's power (the opening of the earth and fire from heaven) to humans is devastating! As bad as the tempting, sinning, and punishment were, however, there were still blessings for the Israelites who did not succumb to evil. In the eyes of all the Israelites, Moses's prediction was realized: "In the morning the Lord will make known who is his, and who is holy, and who will be allowed to approach him" (Num 16:5a). The whole sad episode of Korah's rebellion served to make clear to the Israelites who they were in relation to the Lord and the Lord's holiness.

For many Christian readers, the immediate violence of God's punishment of rebellious Israelites is troubling. It is difficult to square God's self-sacrificial love in Jesus with the fatal discipline of the community when they/we go astray. This is, by no means, a feature of God limited to the Hebrew Bible, as Ananias and Sapphria would testify (Acts 5:1–11). Honestly wrestling with a God who makes us uncomfortable and does not fit neatly into our systematic theologies is, I argue, a sign of a maturing faith. The quote is frequently attributed to Augustine of Hippo that "if you have understood it [and are comfortable with it], it is not God."

> **There is no level of church governance that is immune from those who would seize power.**

There is no level of church governance that is immune from those who would seize power. They, like Korah, are to be resisted with wisdom and fidelity to God, whether they are pastors, congregational council members, synod/diocese staff, or other members of church hierarchy. Remember that the Israelite community saw Moses come out of God's presence; they saw his face supernaturally resplendent from the contact and approval from God. The rabbis said that just as Moses's face shone like the sun after he laid hands on Joshua the son of Nun to be his replacement, so did Joshua's face shine like the moon. They argued that just as one candle is lit from another without the first decreasing in light, so the Israelite elders who had been chosen by Moses and

God for leadership had faces that shone like Moses's after the spirit that rested on Moses was shared with them (Num 11:25).[11] There is a great need for leadership in the church. Moses shared the responsibility with others, and he knew his light would not be diminished by sharing authority with others. My work in the Indiana-Kentucky and Southern Ohio Synods is to train lay leaders to help lead congregations without called rostered ministers. The lay leaders are not a threat to people who have been through seminary, and they do not diminish the calling of others. Instead, they simply work as parts of the Body of Christ to help us all love God and love our neighbor. We should only be concerned when those in power arrogantly pursue power for its own sake instead of as a responsibility to help bless God's people.

But what do we do when the faces of godly leaders and power-hungry usurpers look the same? Later in this chapter, I discuss choosing responsible leaders. Suffice it to say now, when considering a potential leader in the church, we could do worse than consider this Bible text: "For an overseer, as God's steward, must be blameless; (s)he must not be arrogant or quick-tempered or addicted to wine or violent or greedy for gain; but (s)he must be hospitable, a lover of goodness, prudent, upright, devout, and self-controlled. (S)He must have a firm grasp of the word that is trustworthy in accordance with the teaching, so that (s)he may be able both to preach with sound doctrine and to refute those who contradict it" (paraphrase of Titus 1:7–9).

Korah, who maligned God's anointed leader, was not a good candidate for leadership. This is true even if God had not already made clear the limits of his role, which God had. Rather, it was clear to everyone except a few Reubenites that Korah was out for himself. We ought to be similarly cautious in following—or becoming—such power-hungry leaders.

While fleeing from self-aggrandizement and power-hungry leaders, we need to remember that in the body of Christ, just as in the Israelite community, we all have important roles to play. It continues to be important that we all do our part and live up to our full calling. Temptation in the wilderness can keep us from fulfilling the full role that God has called us to, just as it can cause us to overstep our authority. We need to be careful to not let the pendulum swing too far in either direction by grasping authority that is not ours or by shunning authority that God calls us to. As is often the case, Jesus shows us the way.

The Temptation and Testing of Jesus

The tempting of Jesus occurred at a pivotal moment in his ministry. After his baptism by his elder relative John, at which the voice of God commissioned Jesus for his work, he was led into the wilderness to be tempted. This may at first seem a bit odd to modern readers, but it shows continuity with the preceding parts of the Gospel narratives in at least two ways.

The first and most important for our purposes is that it amplifies the official pronouncements of who Jesus is. John the Baptizer told the crowds that Jesus was more powerful than John, whose sandals he was not worthy to carry: "[Jesus] will baptize you with the Holy Spirit and fire" (Matt 3:11). John the Evangelist recorded an even more pointed statement from John the Baptizer upon seeing Jesus: "Behold, the Lamb of God who takes away the sin of the world!" (John 1:29 TLV). Many scholars of Jesus's life suppose that Jesus stayed with and trained with his relative John for a period of time before beginning his own ministry. We cannot be sure what Jesus did in his late youth and early adulthood. In any case, these acclamations from John and the public baptism of Jesus seem to have marked a transition and a sort of graduation ceremony from training and preparation into active ministry. Like any proud parent, God is there to publicly announce favor and, more crucially, to say who Jesus is: "This is my son, whom I love; with him I am well pleased!" (Matt 3:17 NIV).

It is to this series of public acclamations about who Jesus is that the Synoptic Gospel authors add the account of the temptation. Satan began his first two temptations of Jesus with the conditional statement "If you are the Son of God," attempting to put in doubt what God had just declared about Jesus. In resisting the devil's temptation, Jesus confirmed for himself, Satan, and the subsequent readers of the Gospel accounts that Jesus is truly God's son and not in thrall to the evil one at all.

The temptation passage links to the rest of the Gospel by showing that Jesus grew and matured. As Luke 2:52 points out, Jesus grew in wisdom and stature, in favor with God and people. It is frequently helpful to remind ourselves that Jesus was not born fully formed, either physically or mentally. He matured, and this process took place over time through bodily experiences.[12] He was not finished just because his ministry began, but like the full human that he was, he kept growing and changing during his earthly life. The Epistle to the Hebrews points out how important the temptation, and the suffering during it, was to his preparation to intercede with God on our behalf as our high priest: "Therefore he had to become like his brothers and sisters in every respect, so that he might be a merciful and faithful high priest in the service of God, to make a sacrifice of atonement for the sins of the people. Because he himself was tested by what he suffered, he is able to help those who are being tested" (Heb 2:17–18).

Jesus's successful overcoming of temptation is presented as straightforward in the Gospels. But Hebrews tells us that Jesus suffered as he strove to be obedient to God and resist temptation. I cannot imagine not eating for forty days and then having to resist the temptation to provide myself with food!

The nature of the tempting of Jesus was comprehensive. Satan tempted Jesus (1) to turn stones to bread to provide for his own physical hunger, (2) to throw himself down from the temple and demonstrate for all those assembled in the holiest place in the world his unique role and power as God's son (Jesus studiously avoids miracles in or around the temple for the rest of his ministry), and (3) to substitute Satan's plan for God's plan, which would have thwarted Jesus's rescue of humans from the devil's power. Jesus chose obedience to God and identity as God's suffering servant over satisfaction of physical appetites, over social acclaim and recognition, and over the avoidance of a painful, humiliating, and profoundly lonely death. It was this temptation on multiple fronts that allowed the author of Hebrews to claim, "We do not have a high priest who is unable to sympathize with our weaknesses, but we have one *who in every respect has been tempted as we are*, yet without sin" (Heb 4:15; emphasis added).

The temptation of Jesus was a difficult process. It should go without saying, but if what Satan was asking Jesus to do was not on some level attractive to him, the process could hardly be called temptation. But Jesus chose his identity as God's Son over his other desires. God confirmed Jesus's choice by setting him apart as the heavenly high priest forever, according to Hebrews 4:10. Jesus the Messiah's wilderness experience provided an opportunity to figure out and then demonstrate who he was and whose he is! Now we turn back to the Israelite camp in the wilderness to ponder how, even when they were living up to God's hopes for them, they still had opportunities to choose how they would express their identity in the wilderness.

On Choosing and Understanding

A few years ago, I was asked to give a sermon because our pastors were both leaving the country for a few weeks. I prepared for several days, losing writing time on this book, but it came together in the end. I spoke to a couple hundred Christians from a least a score of different countries who lived in Morocco about the hope we have based on Jesus's suffering, death, and resurrection. I thought it went pretty well, but there were mixed reviews, as there always are. My wife, who is a reliable critic and is incapable of pulling punches, said that she cried at a few points in the sermon because of how much God loved her. However bad other people thought the sermon was, if it communicated God's love to my wife, I felt comfortable that God had used me.

But that morning before I stood up and while the congregation was praying afterward, I felt plagued by the question, What am I supposed to be doing the rest of the time? Preparing and preaching sermons is all well and good, but that's not what I spend most of my life doing. I trust and embrace the truth that God, through Jesus, accomplished salvation for us. Living as one of God's beloved, I try to do the daily tasks that God calls me to do, such as giving to those experiencing homelessness, training up my sons, partnering with my wife, preparing to love and honor my students through my teaching, and trying to be a faithful middle manager in the church. But I have felt so convicted, especially as I was preparing to write this section of this chapter, that I am only swimming in the shallows in the wide ocean of God's action in the world.

> I am only swimming in the shallows in the wide ocean of God's action in the world.

This very morning as I was writing these thoughts I was looking at some old notes that I wrote about how the Israelites accepted the covenant at Sinai, and I felt God speak to me through them. Exodus 24:7 says, "Then he [Moses] took the book of the covenant, and read it in the hearing of the people; and they said, 'All that the Lord has spoken we will do, and *nishama*.'" The meaning of this last word, *nishama*, which I have left untranslated, is tremendously impactful to me and my life. Usually this word in this verse is translated into English as "obey." The root *shin/mem/ayin* usually carries a valiance of something like "hear." Many Christians know the Hebrew of Deuteronomy 6:4, *Shema Yisrael*,

"Hear [O] Israel." The roots of *niSHaMA* and *SHeMA* are the same. But that meaning of "hear" does not make much sense in the context of Exodus 24:7. We will *do* and we will *hear*? Hear what? Hearing the law needs to come before doing the law. Similarly, "obey" does not make much sense. Obeying the law should come before or at least at the very same time as the doing. This is possible and is why many chose to translate *nishama* as "obey." However, I argue that there is a better translation.

A commentary on the book of Exodus, *Mekhilta d'Rabbi Shimon bar Yochai*, provides a key insight into our translation quandary. The author argues that *nishama* should be translated according to one of the other possible meanings of the root: "we will *understand*." The work states that when Moses first offered the Torah to the Israelites, they boldly proclaimed, "All that God has said we will do" (Exod 19:8). Some time later, after Moses had begun to detail all the rules and laws that God had for them, the people again exclaimed, "All of the things that God has said, we will do" (Exod 24:3). Finally, after Moses wrote down all the commandments and then read them to the people again, they exclaimed, "*Na'aseh v'nishama* / We will do and [then] we will understand," since they had initially prioritized just doing. Moses asked them, "Can you really do first before you understand? Understanding brings one to doing." The people replied that indeed they would do, and then only after they had done the actions would they understand.

How can we ever understand the meaning and implications of what we do before we do it? We can think we have some idea, and we can predict, but we only understand the significance after an event, if at all. Martin Luther once remarked that when a father washes diapers, though he does not want to do it, "God is smiling . . . not because that father is washing diapers, but because he is doing so in Christian faith."[13] I have come to have the exact same experience. The Israelites wandering around the wilderness faced this challenge—to daily do the small acts that would help them understand their identity as God's chosen people.

"Let No One Deceive You with Empty Words!"

Thinking about how the ancient Israelites faced temptation in the wilderness is valuable and fruitful. But a book about navigating the wildernesses that we face, and especially a chapter on how temptation helps reveal who we are, would be incomplete without at least a few paragraphs dealing with modern temptations. I feel like it is in forging intentional communities and thinking about who our neighbors are and how we want to love them—or not—that temptation may lead us astray from our wilderness journey into maturity and faithfulness with the God who journeys with us. As we seek to apply the lessons of God's word to our lives, we should remember that most of the lessons in the Israelites' wilderness were about community relations and how to recognize God's leadership. Our expression of inclusive community is also a way to enact our core social values to reveal even more clearly than our Sunday morning songs who we are and what we believe. As Dr. Cornel West frequently reminds us, we should "never forget that justice is what love looks like in public."[14]

At least in my upbringing, being on the lookout for sexual temptation and being ready to give a defense of our faith were always primary concerns. But we neglected to exercise the advice of Jesus to be as wise as serpents and as innocent as doves (Matt 10:16) in communal life was neglected. As much as I have come to treasure this commandment of Jesus, I prefer the wording of command to embrace wisdom and reject evil in Ephesians: "Let no one deceive you with empty words, for because of these things the wrath of God comes on those who are disobedient. Therefore do not be associated with them" (Eph 5:6–7).

Plenty of the things we are asked to believe about God seem foolish at first. For me, the wilderness is a time to remember the promises God made and to cling to them even when they seem crazy. I remember how God saved the Israelite people and provided for their needs in the wilderness. This is the opposite of the foolishness I want to address below: the foolishness of forgetting what God has done and said.

As I have mentioned before, the wilderness provides an opportunity to clarify and purify our hearts and minds. Am I believing things that God *did not* say about Godself? About me and my community? About the people around me? Sometimes we are led to folly by believing lies. When we experience the unpleasantness of the unsettling emotional and spiritual wildernesses that can pop up in our everyday lives, we can use the experience to explore feelings and beliefs more deeply and to make changes.

But in this exploration, we must remember that Jesus's goal is a love that includes the unlovable, not a cold righteousness that cuts off all who do not meet certain standards. I have seen family members and close friends marshal Bible verses to demonize those of every other political stripe. This is profoundly sad, I think. It reflects badly on our witness to those who are not Christian. The violence and vitriol of our language undermine Jesus's hope for us that we will be one just as he and the father are one (John 17:22), a mind-blowingly radical kind of unity.

Unity in Wisdom

To that end, I will close this chapter with a call for unity in wisdom and look to the Bible for guidance for avoiding temptation and folly. Scores of times, God's voice through the biblical text urges us to gain and seek wisdom and avoid folly. Frequently these two tasks can be accomplished at the same time. My wife, who works as an international development consultant, applies an important piece of the Hippocratic oath to her own work: first do no harm.

Missionary history and the history of international development and aid provide numerous examples of well-meaning people trying to make a positive difference. Some of them, through a combination of incomplete knowledge of local contexts and that pesky universal inability to accurately predict the future, end up hurting people rather than, or in addition to, helping them. Stepping back, trying to understand the situation better, and returning to a few of Scripture's teachings on community and interpersonal issues will be a tremendous help to us in avoiding similar fates. Accordingly, I want to look at three ways we can avoid deceptive, empty words, in the language of Ephesians 5.

The Fruit and the Tree

At least a couple times in his earthly ministry, Jesus counseled those who follow him to recognize a tree by its fruit. First, he cautions us,

> Beware of false prophets, who come to you in sheep's clothing but inwardly are ravenous wolves. You will know them by their fruits. Are grapes gathered from thorns, or figs from thistles? In the same way, every good tree bears good fruit, but the bad tree bears bad fruit. A good tree cannot bear bad fruit, nor can a bad tree bear good fruit. Every tree that does not bear good fruit is cut down and thrown into the fire. Thus you will know them by their fruits. (Matt 7:15–20)

Second, he says,

> Either make the tree good, and its fruit good; or make the tree bad, and its fruit bad; for the tree is known by its fruit. You brood of vipers! How can you speak good things, when you are evil? For out of the abundance of the heart the mouth speaks. The good person brings good things out of a good treasure, and the evil person brings evil things out of an evil treasure. I tell you, on the day of judgment you will have to give an account for every careless word you utter; for by your words you will be justified, and by your words you will be condemned. (Matt 12:33–37)

What should be common sense has sadly become controversial, and the words of our Lord and Savior are frequently neglected as inconvenient. Words matter and deeds matter. If someone shows you who they are with their deeds and actions, you should believe them. We show others who and whose we are by how we behave toward them.

What I would like to suggest is that we would be better served by considering the fruits of the Spirit in our and our neighbor's lives than by considering social markers or other markers of political affiliation. A person who displays love, joy, peace, patience, kindness, goodness, faithfulness, gentleness, and self-control in life is likely to continue to do so. A person who demonstrates hate, anger, conflict, impatience, mean-spiritedness, corruption, dishonesty, crudeness, and a lack of self-control (the opposites of the fruit of the Spirit) is likely to continue displaying these negative traits.

> We believe in a God who works transformation and resurrection.

We believe in a God who works transformation and resurrection. We should not write off anyone—including ourselves—because of a rough stretch. God is reconciling the world to Godself. But as we look to saints of the past, we can see a community that performed love to neighbor and goodness in community and continued to mature in peace, patience, and self-control. We do not believe that we can improve ourselves by our own will. Instead, we cooperate with the Holy Spirit, who leads and guides us into bearing fruit for the kingdom of heaven.

Neglecting the Weightier Matters

In his earthly ministry and his own wilderness wandering as he preached and taught, Jesus encountered many religious folks who were frequently in danger of majoring in minors—that is, focusing on less important things and neglecting more important issues: "Woe to you, scribes and Pharisees, hypocrites! For you tithe mint, dill, and cummin, and have neglected the weightier matters of the law: justice and mercy and faith. It is these you ought to have practiced without neglecting the others. You blind guides! You strain out a gnat but swallow a camel!" (Matt 23:23–24).

Jesus spells out for us the weightier matters of the law. They are justice, mercy, and faithfulness. And yet how many of our daily decisions are made by thinking about justice, let alone mercy and faithfulness? How many of us sit down and, before we speak with our spouses or children, examine if what we are asking our families to do is just, merciful, and faithful to our God and to our brothers and sisters? I certainly wish I would think more about justice, mercy, and faithfulness as I try to move forward in wilderness times of uncertainty and disorientation. Instead, more often, I think about what I can do to bring personal comfort and normalcy. Christians can and do disagree about what is just and faithful, of course. But we can start to bridge disagreements in our families and communities by discussing how we are moved and guided by common motivations and values.

As an example of consistent guidance toward justice, mercy, and faithfulness during wilderness times, no fewer than thirty-six times in the biblical text, God's people are told to be kind to the foreigner living among them because they themselves were foreigners in Egypt. The New Testament is a story of God's community expanding to include gentiles, foreigners to laws and customs, with a gracious welcome. Welcoming the foreigner is among the most-often repeated instructions in the Bible, right up there with "do not fear" and "praise God." This commandment demands a radical double dose of empathy. First, we need to be empathetic to our ancestors, who themselves were foreigners (unless we are First Nation, or Indigenous, peoples, of course). The Israelites heard this commandment after the first wilderness generation had died off; this generation had not experienced being foreigners in Egypt. And yet the descendants of those generations were told that they were to welcome the foreigner because they themselves had been foreigners. We who can trace our ancestry, even many generations later, to some prior place (most people in the world probably fall into this category) are still foreigners, according to the word of God. We are called to embrace and experience the feelings of our ancestors as they left home and, not knowing what was before them, came to a new land. The narrative of Judges presents a relatively weak group of Israelites who were repeatedly abused in their new home with only periodic relief. Many of our own ancestors were abused when they left famine, war, and poverty to arrive in their new homes or were forcibly enslaved and brought to new homes against their will. With this commandment, God assumes we will be thoughtful and empathetic enough to think about how they would have liked to have been treated and act that way toward others.

The second kind of empathy demanded is empathy and mercy we show the foreigners we face in modern life. We are to welcome the foreigner—not merely tolerate, not grudgingly accept, certainly not refuse, but welcome them. In so doing, we fulfill not just the thirty-six times we are commanded to welcome the foreigner because we were foreigners but also the commandment to do unto others as we would want done unto ourselves. In a wilderness moment when we do not

Mercy invites us to forgive the transgressions of others.

know the way forward, especially with regard to the immigration of foreigners, justice demands that we practice the gracious welcome we would like to receive for ourselves in a foreign land. Mercy invites us to forgive the transgressions of others. And faithfulness requires that we look to God first and foremost for our orientation in confusing situations. God's story is about how to faithfully love God in part through loving and including foreigners. The point of the story of the Good Samaritan was not that Samaritans were good but that even the hated Samaritans were neighbors to be loved (Luke 10:29, 36). The weightier matters of the law are loving and welcoming people, especially when it is difficult, confusing, and perhaps even unsafe.

Favoring the Rich or the Poor

Just as there is to be one fair standard applied to the native born and the foreign born (Exod 12:49; Lev 24:22; Num 15:29; etc.), there is to be one fair standard that applies to everyone, irrespective of financial situation. A few times in Scripture, we are instructed to apply justice fairly: "Do not pervert justice; do not show partiality to the poor or favoritism to the great, but judge your neighbor fairly" (Lev 19:15 NIV) and "Do not show favoritism to a poor person in a lawsuit" (Exod 23:3 NIV). Before we move on, it should be noted that only three verses later in Exodus, we are told not to deprive the poor of justice in their lawsuits either.

So why this concern? It is not as if, for instance, the poor in society are in danger of taking over and we really need God to tell people not to help them. The temptation to side with the little guy is frequently strong and tugs at our hearts. On the other end of the scale, who can deny the societal "wisdom" of ingratiating oneself with a rich and powerful patron who may be able to return the favor? The temptation to side with the poor or with the rich/great is very real. And this is a shame. Let me explain.

Few things are more corrosive to unity in a society than unequal application of the laws. Even the mere hint of the law being in favor of the other, whether rich or poor, is enough to fuel distrust and division. While it is true that in the United States, the poor disproportionally benefit from government assistance and entitlement programs, the rich disproportionally benefit from infrastructure spending, municipal investments, bailouts, and tax breaks. But I do not think these are the foci of the biblical injunctions. Rather, I understand the commandments to be focused on the juridical and interpersonal spheres.

As we stand before the judge—and here I am talking about in an earthly courtroom—we have an expectation, or at least a desire, that the facts of the case will be the only thing under consideration. We know, however, that that simply is not the case. The Sentencing Project, an American NGO, demonstrated in its 2013 report to the United Nations that "the United States operates two distinct criminal justice systems: one for wealthy people and another for poor people and minorities."[15] It will come as absolutely no surprise to anyone that conviction rates for the wealthy, who are able to afford better legal help than a public defender overwhelmed with cases, are much lower.

An estimated 450,000 people are in jail every day *awaiting trial*.[16] That is to say, people who are innocent until proven guilty, whose trials have not even begun, are in jail, mostly because they were too poor to post bail. In the state of Maryland alone, where I am writing this chapter, between 2011 and 2015, 80,000 people went to jail because they could not afford bail or a bond, and of those, 17,000 were in jail with a bail amount of less than $5,000.[17] To have a system that jails poor people before they are convicted of anything simply because they are not rich enough or do not have sufficient credit to be afforded a bond is clearly unjust.

It is not just in the judicial system that we differentiate between the rich and poor. In the broad senses of "judging" from Leviticus 19, we show "partiality" and "favor" every day by whom we associate with. James, the head of the Jerusalem church and the brother of Jesus, warned about economically based favoritism: "My brothers and sisters, believers in our glorious Lord Jesus Christ must not show favoritism. Suppose a man comes into your meeting wearing a gold ring and fine clothes, and a poor man in filthy old clothes also comes in. If you show special attention to the man wearing fine clothes and say, 'Here's a good seat for you,' but say to the poor man, 'You stand there' or 'Sit on the floor by my feet,' have you not discriminated among yourselves and become judges with evil thoughts?" (Jas 2:1–4 NIV).

James was certainly more concerned that the people would show favoritism to the rich than to the poor, but the last sentence makes clear that favoritism to anyone is not to be tolerated. Thus in our communities we are to practice a radical egalitarianism, according to James, even in positionality.

Do we cluster ourselves in a fancy restaurant, or do we shun the rich and only dine on park benches and curbs? Both. Neither. I am not sure. I think what is important is that we interrogate our choices about whom we surround ourselves with, whom we prefer, whom we are open to meeting, and whom we deem "the other." Again, Jesus is a good example because he associated with the poor, the diseased, the pagan (Romans, Canaanites, and Samaritans), the rich, the spiritual leadership, and political rulers (there was quite a bit of overlap between the last two categories).

Many well-meaning Christians will embrace the poor and downtrodden because they are blessed by Jesus. Good! It is right that we should do so. But when that embrace turns to favoritism or prohibits a complete embrace of the rich siblings in Christ, it becomes sinful. Likewise, many Christians embrace the rich for their abundance (potentially God given) and for their willingness to endow congregations and churches. That is OK, too, I think, until it causes the poor to be treated as less important than everyone else. Instead, in an uncertain wilderness in which we are attempting to move forward in faithfulness, we need to learn how to ask the right questions to understand our neighbors and to withhold judgment until we come to see our neighbors as the dearly beloved children of God who they are. Above all, we are to love our neighbors and work toward justice for those who are being oppressed. I think anything else is a distraction on our wilderness journey.

In the wilderness, temptation is all around us. This is not to be feared but rather embraced. It affords us the opportunity to show God, our community, and ourselves who we really are. We have the opportunity to shun temporary enticements, lust for power, and fear of others in favor of choosing to identify as children of the God who saves us all. In all of that, we must avoid empty words and embrace wisdom. However, if we only think of ourselves and who/whose we are, we miss another crucial part of what God is doing in the wilderness: giving us a vision of what is to come!

GUIDED REFLECTIONS

1. How can we be wise in discerning temptation? Just as Balaam wasn't able to curse the Israelites directly but then used sexual temptation that led to idolatry, sometimes a successful defense leads to an attack from another direction. Where are your weak spots, and how can you receive help from God and trusted friends to avoid becoming sidetracked on your wilderness journey?

2. Do you long for advancement of position and power? Why? Certainly God calls many of God's people to leadership and many to humble supporting roles. For those in leadership roles, how can we emulate the good shepherd who laid down his life for the sheep?

For those in following roles, how can we support those in positions of authority and serve others? If, as is likely, you find yourself in leadership and following roles in different contexts, how can you be the kind of leader and follower that you would like to follow and lead, respectively?

3. Is it a new concept to you that Jesus's temptation was difficult for him and caused him to suffer? If the Son of God suffered during temptation, how does this free you up to talk with trusted community members about your own difficult temptations? Facing temptation is difficult, even for the Messiah!

4. Avoiding foolish ideas is all well and good, but how do we do positive things instead? My wise mother-in-law suggested a practice that I love: Before every election (in government or at church), think of four or five policy goals that you have for whomever you are voting for that reflect justice, mercy, and faithfulness. Write them down and then think on those goals to remind yourself and others of what you really care about.

5. What actions can you take in your life that express justice, mercy, and faithfulness, the weightier matters of the law?

3

Place of Vision: Where God Is Leading

Then the Lord answered me and said:

Write the vision;
  make it plain on tablets,
  so that a runner may read it.

—Habakkuk 2:2

More than any other place, the wilderness experience that rips us from our daily routine is where God speaks to us. This is because the wilderness is a weird place, in which our weird/holy God gives us weird/countercultural words. Why should we not expect this? The story of God's people has been a story of turning aside from settled places and normal life.

The biblical text is rife with stories of God's people leaving the normal behind and embracing the weird/holy/unknown, where they encountered God and received a vision for their futures.

Noah turned aside from his normal routine to do a deeply weird thing: build a giant box boat because he heard from God about an impending flood. The patriarchs moved from their home environment to a new land, the land to which God called them. And the matriarchs, no less than their husbands, and in some cases rather more dramatically, answered the call to go into the wilderness not only geographically but socially and spiritually as they left their natal families. Sarah, Rebekah, Leah, and Rachel (along with Hagar, Bilhah, and Zilpah, who had less choice in the matter) all left their homes and their people to journey to a place unknown. Remember that Sarah and Hagar conversed directly with angels and God as they journeyed! All of these women and men saw the works of God, mostly in terms of family provision, because they left their normal lives and responded to God calling them to an unsettled life. Their experiences of hearing God in the wilderness serve as a pattern for God's people ever after.

Many of us feel enlivened while "communing with nature." For most of us, our daily, routine lives are not spent in nature. Many of us spend so much time in our work cubicles or apartments that when we can get out into nature even in the neighborhood, it can sometimes feel weird. Weird as in holy. I dare say that the God of the universe who created the mountains, forests, and oceans also created our hearts to long for them. It is in these places that we are far enough away from our daily concerns that we can more easily silence ourselves and hear the word of the Lord. But that is only a geographic wilderness. More often, we experience moments of wonder when we have a peculiar or novel experience right where we live. When the strange, weird, or holy breaks through our sense of what is normal or expected, we suddenly find ourselves in a wilderness moment, even in the midst of the city. And it is then and there, frequently, that we hear most clearly from God.

Just as God is calling us to a place where we can be intimate with our maker, so God called the first human. Avivah Gottlieb Zornberg, a scholar whose work focuses on Rashi's Bible interpretation and human psychology, gives an achingly beautiful description of a midrash concerning Genesis 2:15:

> "The Lord God took the man and put him in the garden of Eden to till it and keep it": "He [Rashi] uses Midrash a great deal, so he has this wonderful comment on the word 'and God took him.' His implication, what's behind it, is that how do you take a human being? You can take an object and move it from here to there, but how do you take a human being? And he [Rashi] says, 'He [God] seduced him with words. He seduced him with beautiful words.'"[1]

God seduces us with God's creation to call us to a place where we can be together. On the face of it, that may sound scandalous. But that is exactly what happens in the biblical text over and over. For example, Hebrews 11 points to many who followed God by faith into new places. They were enticed to follow God by hopes unseen. On the occasions when God commands us to leave our ordinary lives, we do it because we know that obedience to God is sweet and winsome, even when it involves giving up everything we have known.

I have come to understand chosen wilderness times as taking two forms: (1) withdrawing from normal life for quiet, solitude, listening, prayer, renewal, and so on or (2) choosing to go "outside

the camp" to identify with those who are oppressed, poor, persecuted, and so on. In both cases, we catch a vision of what God is
doing in our own lives and in the lives of those for whom God
expresses special care. These wilderness times that are chosen
intentionally can be incredibly fruitful. They help us go deeper
into relationship with God with both a sustainable relational
foundation and a fast track to God's heart and presence.

> **These
> wilderness times
> that are chosen
> intentionally can
> be incredibly
> fruitful.**

Forced wilderness experiences,
however, are times of bewilderment,
confusion, anger, rejection, and clar-
ification. In the wilderness, we are
given opportunities to evaluate our
beliefs. We see whether we can hold
on to a view that is true ultimately but
difficult to maintain in the moment or
whether this is a time to reform beliefs we had previously taken
for granted. Forced wilderness experiences—such as the loss of
a job, the death of a loved one, or the breakup of an important
relationship—can be times of remembering and holding tight to
the promises of God and times of letting the wind blow away the
chaff in our lives. We can benefit from the difficult struggles
through questions that lead us to the unshakable truth of God's
intimacy with us, especially in wilderness times.

As profoundly different as these kinds of wilderness experiences are, however, I believe that they all can be fruitful. Whether
God entices us out to the wilderness with the allure of holy/weird
beauty, or we are chased out of our preferred ways of thinking,
feeling, and being and encounter God by accident, God waits for

us in the lonely places and longs to give us a vision of what God is doing in the world and in our lives.

Seeing God's Presence

More than any other people in the history of this world, the Israelites in the desert camp had a daily visual assurance of God's presence: the pillar of smoke and fire. Throughout Scripture, God chose to signify God's personal presence by means of smoke (see Gen 15:17–21; Exod 19:18; Isa 6:4; and Rev 15:8). This smoke was a clear sign that God, who is Lord of the entire universe, had chosen to focus a special amount of divine attention and presence at a certain place and time in human history. There were three main purposes for God appearing in the pillar of smoke in the wilderness camp. The first function of the visual presence of the Lord in the pillar of cloud and fire was to instruct the Israelites on when and where to journey: "Whenever the cloud lifted from over the tent, then the Israelites would set out; and in the place where the cloud settled down, there the Israelites would camp. At the command of the Lord the Israelites would set out, and at the command of the Lord they would camp. As long as the cloud rested over the tabernacle, they would remain in camp" (Num 9:17–18). The people's entire agenda for over forty years was looking to the presence of God for guidance. If the visual manifestation of God's presence was in the midst of the camp, then the people stayed around God's pillar. If the locus of God's presence moved and went ahead of them, the people followed until they had encircled the pillar of cloud, and then they set up God's tent again. In this manner, God led God's people through the wilderness daily.

The second purpose of the pillar of smoke and fire was to publicly cement Moses as God's chosen leader and to confirm his ongoing favor with the Lord. Moses regularly went into the tent of meeting to speak with the Lord (Num 7:89), but on a few occasions, the pillar of cloud came down to speak with Moses in the sight of the people. The first instance was in a public commissioning of godly elders: "So Moses went out and told the people the words of the Lord; and he gathered seventy elders of the people, and placed them all around the tent. Then the Lord came down in the cloud and spoke to him, and took some of the spirit that was on him and put it on the seventy elders; and when the spirit rested upon them, they prophesied. But they did not do so again" (Num 11:24–25). The public appearance of the cloud and the voice that spoke with Moses confirmed not only the ordination of the elders but also Moses's ongoing leadership.

God's affirmation of the call on Moses's life, again from the pillar of cloud, is made even clearer as Moses's siblings complained against him:

> Then the Lord came down in a pillar of cloud, and stood at the entrance of the tent, and called Aaron and Miriam; and they both came forward. And he said, "Hear my words:
>
> When there are prophets among you,
>> I the Lord make myself known to them in visions;
>> I speak to them in dreams.

Not so with my servant Moses;
>   he is entrusted with all my house.
With him I speak face to face—clearly, not in riddles;
>   and he beholds the form of the Lord.

Why then were you not afraid to speak against my servant
Moses?" (Num 12:5–8)

God confirmed the existence of other prophets, and God appeared to them in visions. In this way, all the Israelites could have been considered prophets because of their daily sight of God's presence as manifested in the pillar. But Moses was in another class entirely. Not only did Moses speak with God face-to-face, but God publicly and dramatically confirmed Moses's special status with God. His role as leader was confirmed to the Israelite community by means of deploying the pillar of fire and smoke. Would that we had the pillar of cloud in our days to demonstrate who is a faithful leader! This would certainly have helped prevent many crises of abusive leadership in our churches.

The third use of the pillar of cloudy smoke was to send a message to the surrounding peoples who were potential enemies of the wandering wilderness camp. The presence of God signified to all those who did not happen to have a pillar of cloud and fire dwelling in the midst of their community that the Israelites were a community set apart for the God who saved them: "Moses said to the Lord, 'Then the Egyptians will hear of it, for in your might you brought up this people from among them, and they will tell the inhabitants of this land. They have heard that you, O Lord, are in the midst of this people; for you, O Lord, are seen face to face, and your cloud stands over them and you go in front of them, in a pillar of cloud by day and in a pillar of fire by night'" (Num 14:13–14). The Egyptians had suffered greatly at the hands of God, who exacted vengeance on them for their inhumanity toward the Hebrews. In these verses, Moses insinuated that the Egyptians would be quick to warn other peoples not to trifle with the God of Israel, lest they suffer the same fate as the Egyptians. We should not forget that after exiting Egypt proper but before crossing the Reed Sea, the pillar of God acted as a rear guard for the Israelites to prevent the slow-moving, massive column of civilians from being overrun by the Egyptian army (Exod 14:19–20).

One can imagine the people of the land, such as King Balak, growing increasingly nervous at seeing a massive group of people on the border with a pillar of cloud by day and fire by night in their midst. As if that were not enough to frighten the people of the land, an ancient commentary described the pillar "killing snakes and scorpions, burning up thorns, thistles, and underbrush, flattening the high places and straightening valleys, thereby making the way straight for them" (Tosefta Sotah 4:2). Anyone who has spent days hiking and climbing around the Sinai can attest that such divine intervention would have been welcome. Imagine how terrifying the pillar of cloud and fire would have been to the peoples who encountered the wandering Israelites.

Even before the wilderness journey, however, God provided ample signs of God's power and attention while the Israelites were still slaves in Egypt. After the Israelites entered the Holy Land, during the conquest narratives of Joshua and Judges, God again provided miracles and signs as the Israelites attempted to subdue the land. But the pillar of cloud that demonstrated God's presence among God's people was a daily fixture only during the wilderness times. Again, God was certainly with the people before and after the wilderness wandering, but the vision of God's presence was only available in the wilderness. We do not know exactly when the pillar stopped being a daily presence in the lives of the Israelites, but we do have a pretty good idea that it was when the people were on the cusp of entering the land of milk and honey.

Numbers 33 gives the account of all the campsites from which the Israelites departed at God's command. The last of these campsites was on the banks of the Jordan River in the plains of Moab. This last recorded spot was the end of the narrative of God leading the people by the pillar of cloud and fire; this is probably when they stopped seeing it daily. Just four days after the Israelites finally crossed the river under Joshua's leadership, the miraculous provision of manna that they had eaten in the wilderness stopped (Josh 5:12). An account in the Talmud (Ta'anit 9b) says that the pillar of cloud and fire ceased on the day that Aaron died, around Mount Hor, a bit to the south of where the Jordan River enters the Dead Sea. At any rate, somewhere by the Jordan River, near the borders of the land, as the Israelites left the wilderness, they lost their daily vision of God's presence. As they entered the land, they left a wilderness and entered the territory of Jericho, one of the oldest urban centers on the planet.

Again, this is not to say that God stopped being present in any way. God was not any less intimate, but there is an important difference between being able to use one's senses to verify the presence of God and just having to know and trust that God is faithful. I was just talking with my wife about the first time that I moved back to the United States from Morocco a few months before I first met her. I moved to an unfamiliar city to be close to a woman whom I did not know well. Soon, it became clear that I should not have further interactions with her. I was alone in a city where I knew no one, didn't have a job, and had recently signed a lease with rent due every month.

Months of loneliness and doubt followed. I was hemorrhaging money and beating myself up for how I dove headfirst into a bad situation. (Love letters are trouble if you don't really know the person with whom you are corresponding!) I had been applying for jobs for months, with no good leads. In desperation, I prayed to God, "If I am supposed to stay here, I'm going to need a sign of your presence. Otherwise, I'm moving back in with my parents!" The next day, I heard back from a job that I had applied for earlier but did not have much faith that I would secure. I was hired! Also, the job provided funding for the master's program that I wanted to pursue. And I met Sarah, who is now my wife. Over a period of a couple weeks, God visibly turned my life around. I had a job, a future, and a new friend (who would be much more than a friend over the coming years). God's presence was manifest. But then, as happens, life created a new normal.

Due to an incorrectly processed tax form, my wages were garnished (but eventually paid back). Working and going to school full time at the same time was a pressure cooker. Like all relationships, dating the woman who would become my wife involved rough spots. All through those times when I could not see God as clearly as I had that one shining week, I had to remember that God was no less present, even though God's actions were less perceptible. I thought I had left the true wilderness and entered normal life. But unsettling and disorienting wildernesses with their confusions and setbacks abounded. God was still with me, but it was in the depths of the wilderness that I really saw a vision of God working.

In the same way, the Israelites' ability to see daily physical manifestations of God's presence ceased when they left the wilderness and entered the promised land. But they would still perceive God's presence with them, nonetheless. Leading the Israelites to their new/ancestral home had been the goal when the wilderness camp was established forty years earlier. It was good to finally move on from the wilderness. The Israelites transitioned from a bunch of freed slaves and the mixed multitude who joined them as they left Egypt (Exod 12:38) to a massive, conquering community.

One of the principal benefits of time spent with God in the wilderness is gaining the freedom to move on.

One of the principal benefits of time spent with God in the wilderness is gaining the freedom to move on from that which troubles us to that which delights God. After we have seen a vision of God and God's plans in our wilderness time, it is right and good to move on and get back to normalcy without letting go of what we have learned and who we have become. It would not have been wise for me to hold on to the wilderness of unemployment, loneliness, and confusion when God was gifting me with a blessed normalcy. The need to move on, however, does nothing to lessen the fact that God is, and has always been, especially willing to give visions of God's presence in the wilderness. Receiving an accurate picture of God, our neighbors, and ourselves often hinges on our level of humility and readiness to focus on the reality of what God is doing.

Not Seeing God

Balaam provides an example of what can prevent us from fulfilling God's vision in the wilderness. When Balaam received his third and fourth visions in Numbers 24, he opened his prophetic speech by praising himself:

> The oracle of Balaam son of Beor,
>   the oracle of the man whose eye is clear,
> the oracle of one who hears the words of God,
>   who sees the vision of the Almighty,
>   who falls down, but with eyes uncovered.
>   (Num 24:3b–4)

When I begin teaching my seminary classes, one of the first things I do is introduce myself, provide a brief professional résumé, discuss how long I have taught Hebrew Bible courses, and review my academic training and influences. If the students are going to value what I say, they should know a bit about the source of the lesson I am about to give them. Balaam was doing for King Balak the same thing that I do for my students. King Balak, who up to this moment had been a very unsatisfied customer of Balaam's prophetic work, was not impressed with Balaam. The problem with Balaam's self-praise was that he was not actually a man whose "eye is clear" or "whose eyes are uncovered."

When we return to the donkey incident of Numbers 22, we see a more accurate picture of Balaam's skills in discerning the actions of what God is doing. The ass had a more complete picture of the spiritual realm than did Balaam. Balaam was oblivious to the vision of the threatening angel that the beast of burden saw. When the Lord opened the donkey's mouth to speak, the question was not "Why didn't you, a seer, see the angel intent on killing you?" but "After you have ridden me your whole life and I have never misbehaved, why didn't you trust me?" This exchange is extremely strange, but it is also telling. The ass knew Balaam his whole life and was not surprised at him missing a fairly crucial detail of an angel blocking their path.

Not only was Balaam more spiritually blind than his ass, but he demonstrated a tendency to abuse those who had done him no harm. Balaam sought to kill his donkey who served him faithfully. He sought to destroy the Israelites who had done him no wrong. In both cases, Balaam was not a man who saw but one who could not see what God was doing without God's direct intervention.

Chapter 24 opens with language that concentrates on eyes and the act of seeing. The passage contrasts the eyes and sight of God with those of Balaam: "When Balaam saw that it was good in the eyes of the Lord to bless Israel, he did not go, as at other times, to look for omens, but turned his face toward the wilderness. And Balaam lifted up his eyes, and saw Israel encamping tribe by tribe. And the Spirit of God came upon him" (Num 24:1–2; my translation). Balaam was finally able to see something of God. He saw that it was good in the Lord's eyes to bless Israel. "Good in the eyes" is a Hebrew idiom that means something like "pleased" or "found favor." But the "eye" and "seeing" language is, I believe, an intentional choice of the inspired writer of the text to contrast how God sees and how Balaam saw.

God looks with blessing and favor on God's people. Balaam did not. Balaam's response to seeing that God was pleased with the Israelites was to desist from seeking omens, which he had apparently been doing up to this point. Balaam also turned and *set his face toward the wilderness* and saw the Israelite camp. He turned from the wasteland/*yeshemon* where King Balak had pointed him (Num 23:28) to the wilderness/*midbar* where the Israelites camped. Balaam changed his orientation, as it were, from looking where King Balak would have him look to looking to God. He no longer looked for omens but to where the Israelites were camping with God. At long last, Balaam turned from the desolate place to look at the wilderness. The wilderness was—and continues to be—where God encamps with God's people.

Upon making this fundamental realignment from looking at his own spiritual perspective to simply seeing what God was actually doing (though he claimed to be doing this all along), Balaam restated his résumé:

> The oracle of Balaam son of Beor,
>   the oracle of the man whose eye is clear,
> the oracle of one who hears the words of God,
>   who sees the vision of the Almighty,

who falls down, but with eyes uncovered.
(Num 24:3b–4)

Balaam was at least partly correct at this point in the story. He had fallen down, as in the episode with his donkey when his eyes were uncovered. The word we translate as "uncovered" here occurs 188 times in the biblical text and usually means something like "forcefully strip/uncover" and carries a connotation of shamefulness. Thus when Balaam admitted that his eyes had been uncovered, he was saying that God had forcefully stripped away the covering of his eyes and (possibly) shamed him by doing so.

What is less clear is what the word we translate as "clear" actually means. The Hebrew word *shatam* is what is called in biblical studies a *dis legomenon*, which is to say it only appears twice in the whole Bible. What makes the word's meaning difficult to ascertain is that both times it occurs in the Bible are in this chapter, in identical sentences.

What is even more curious than the adjective is the number of eyes that are *shatam*. The verse literally says, "*Shatam* [is] the eye." This led to the Talmudic understanding that Balaam had two eyes, but only one of them worked, and he was blind in the other (Sanhedrin 105a). Another rabbinic text (the fifth chapter of Pirkei Avot) used the notion of Balaam's partial blindness to explain a contrast between Balaam and his disciples on the one hand and Abraham and his disciples on the other. The true descendants of Abraham have a good eye, a humble disposition, and a meek spirit. Balaam's disciples, on the contrary, are those who have an evil eye, a haughty bearing, and an avaricious spirit. Those with an evil eye rejoice when others suffer and regret the success of others. The connection between a bad eye and jealousy was so intense in the ancient Near East that, for example, most versions of Mark 7:22 render the Greek, which literally says "evil eye," as simply "envy." The implication is that Balaam had one good/clear eye, but the other eye was evil. That is to say, he was full of jealousy.

But of what or whom was Balaam envious? The short answer is everyone. Before he agreed to go with Balak's men, Balaam mentioned in passing that he would be willing to accept Balak's entire house of silver and gold as payment (Num 22:18), indicating that he was envious of Balak's fortune.[2] But for the sake of the Numbers narrative, Balaam was most jealous of the Israelite people—especially Moses, who did not have to perform elaborate rituals to have a chance to encounter God. For the Israelites, God came to dwell among them as a matter of divine prerogative. Certainly there were rituals involved in the upkeep of tabernacle service, but the God of the Israelites was not a come-and-go God who had to be summoned. The priests and the elders of the Israelite camp had picnics with God in which they saw God (Exod 24:9–11). God was present daily in the camp, and every Israelite saw the manifestation of God's intimacy (Exod 24:17). How galling to be a professional seer whose revelation of God is less dependable than that of the least honorable and important person in the Israelite camp!

What are we to learn from the story of Balaam, who held himself up as one whose eyes are uncovered? I think we would do well to concentrate on the differences between Abraham's descendants and Balaam's. First, Balaam had an evil eye, as opposed to Abraham's good eye(s). Balaam did not want others to be blessed.

Even after God used him as a conduit to bless the Israelites, Balaam found a sneaky way to make sure many of them forfeited their blessings and instead embraced idolatry. Abraham, on the other hand, was known for his generosity to his visitors (Gen 18), his neighbors (Gen 14), his nephew (Gen 13), and his sons (Gen 25:6). Indeed, God said that the nations would be blessed through Abraham's descendants (Gen 22:18). The first way we can learn from the story of Balaam is to see the blessing others receive as blessings to us as well and not as threats. God's love and blessings are not a zero-sum game where we automatically receive less as others gain more. When God chooses to bless someone else, we should rejoice with them rather than seek to deprive them of their favor, as Balaam did to the Israelites. As we come out of the wilderness into a place where we return to a regular, orderly life, we should be careful to imitate Abraham's generosity and not Balaam's jealousy.

The second lesson of Balaam is not to be prideful. Balaam bragged that he was a man with a clear eye, whose eyes were uncovered. Yet his donkey saw the spiritual realm more clearly than he. Balaam exulted himself and used his intellect to curse others, even after blessing them. He was ultimately killed for it (Josh 13:22). Abraham, to the contrary, though a very rich man, acted as a servant to all who came to visit or request his help; again, consider the three visitors or the rescue of Lot. As we exit the wilderness, we do well when we use our gifts and skills to bless God and God's people rather than build up a name for ourselves as Balaam did.

Rejecting the proud and envious "vision" of Balaam in favor of humble gratitude for the presence of God in our midst, especially as we move forward from our wilderness places, carries an abundant blessing. The rabbis' advice to emulate Abraham rather than Balaam squares nicely with the Beatitudes in which Jesus pronounces the poor in spirit, the mourners, the meek, the hungry, the merciful, the pure in heart, the peacemakers, and those who suffer to be particularly blessed (Matt 5:1–11).

As we seek God's vision for how to move forward in the wilderness, we do well not to be prideful or envious. But we also need to bear faithful witness to the vision God shows us. The biblical text is replete with several positive examples of prophets in the wilderness who guide us away from the example of Balaam. These prophets cling to telling God's truths and working to make God's vision a reality.

The Wilderness as a Reservoir of God's Prophetic Spirit

During the time of the monarchs, alongside human leaders who ruled the Israelites, a band of wilderness prophets came to testify and prophesy wisdom and truth. The chief purpose of these prophetic troops, indeed, seems to have been to confirm the leaders' actions when they acted according to the way of the Lord and to speak truth to power when leaders strayed from the right path. The prophetic bands provided visions of what God expected from the leaders of God's people.

The first mention we have of a mass prophetic occasion is, unsurprisingly, from the book of Numbers as the Israelites wandered about in the wilderness. Numbers 11 discusses how the spirit that God had given to Moses was shared with seventy elders of the Israelite community. The elders were appointed and anointed with the spirit that had been given to Moses so that they could handle some of Moses's leadership burdens. The seventy elders prophesied in front of the assembled people as a means to testify to their spiritual authority, derived from the same spiritual authority entrusted to Moses. The text is careful to point out that these elders only prophesied once, however.

By the end of the period of the judges, when Israel cried out for a human king, prophetic bands roving the wilderness seem to have been fairly common. When Samuel anointed Saul to be king, one of the signs of his kingship is that he would meet a band of prophets coming down from an enemy-controlled cultic worship sight, and he would be overcome with a spirit of prophecy. When Samuel instructed Saul as to what signs he would encounter, he did not seem unfamiliar with the idea of a prophetic troop. Moreover, the people who encountered Saul prophesying were only surprised that he was among the prophets, not that prophetic bands existed or that they were able to cross frontiers between friendly and hostile territory. So strange was it for a king to be part of the group that affirmed and challenged his power that "Is Saul also among the prophets?" became a common proverb (1 Sam 10:11). Sometime between the wilderness wanderings and the dawn of the monarchy, wandering prophetic bands became a well-known phenomenon within Israel.

The principal activity of these wandering bands, as mentioned, seems to have been to provide visions and wise guidance to kings. Samuel presided over the meetings of the prophets (1 Sam 19:20), counseled Saul during his reign, and critiqued his misrule (1 Sam 15, for example). The power of the prophetic spirit that characterized the meetings of the prophetic band was infectious, and even the messengers that Saul sent to capture David as he ran from Saul joined the "prophetic frenzy." Even Saul, who by this point had been denounced for his disobedience to God, was overcome by a spirit of prophecy, stripped naked, and lay in a prophetic frenzy for a whole day (1 Sam 19:24).

Saul was not the only king of Israel or Judah to receive messages from the prophetic bands. Nathan, a trusted advisor of David, seems to have been at least a part-time wandering prophet. In 2 Samuel 7:5 and 2 Samuel 12:1, God commands Nathan not just to give David a message but to travel in order to do so. Nathan spent time in the court of King David to be sure. But he did not reside there full time. He was sent back to the court for blessing and critiquing the king, as David's actions deserved.

During the reign of King Ahab of Israel, Jezebel, his Sidonian wife, embarked on a plan to annihilate the prophetic bands who remained faithful to the Lord. Obadiah, a palace servant, separated the prophets into two groups, hid them in caves, and provided food for them (1 Kgs 18:4, 13). Only the leader of the prophetic troops at that time, Elijah, dared speak to King Ahab. Another time, during a war with Ahab and Israel on one side and Ben-Hadad and the Arameans on the other, several prophets advised him on military tactics (1 Kgs 20:13, 22, 28). When the battle was over, however, another member of a prophetic company acted out a strange prophetic performance to declare that Ahab had acted incorrectly in sparing Ben-Hadad's life and that he would pay with his own life (1 Kgs 20:35–43).

The strangest encounter between Ahab and the prophets is told in 1 Kings 22. Ahab made plans with Jehoshaphat, the king of the Southern Kingdom of Judah, to fight as an allied front against the Arameans. Verse 6 points out that Ahab gathered about four hundred prophets together in order to inquire about the success of his planned mission. Though they were beholden to what Ahab wanted to hear, these prophets were still at least nominally in service of the God of the Israelites, as they spoke on behalf of God's divine name and had Israelite names (1 Kgs 22:11–12).

In this prophetic gathering, Jehoshaphat exercised uncommon discernment and was uncomfortable with these prophets, however. He asked if there was another prophet of the Lord who could be consulted. Micaiah then gave his famous account of God holding court with all the angels and spirits. God sought a heavenly being to convince Ahab that war was a good idea so that he would be killed. One spirit volunteered, and God asked the spirit how it planned to entice the king of Israel to battle. The spirit volunteered to be *a lying spirit in the mouth of all his prophets!* God replied, "Go out and do it" (1 Kgs 22:22). Apparently only Micaiah was impervious to the lying spirit and even told the two kings about the conversation between God and the spirit in heaven. His prophecy was chosen against, however, and King Ahab did indeed die in the battle for Ramoth-Gilead. We can feel sympathy for the prophets who were deceived in this case, but such is frequently the fate of those with a prophetic voice who spend too much time in the halls of power and are co-opted by it. They become deceived and need to hear a fresh voice from the wilderness.

The prophetic bands continued to be the source of bad news for the house of Ahab. Elisha dispatched a member of one of his prophetic bands to surreptitiously anoint Jehu king of Israel (2 Kgs 9:1–3). The prophet journeyed to the camp at Ramoth-Gilead and, upon being granted a private audience with Jehu, dumped a flask of oil on his head and proclaimed him king. The prophet then quickly fled. Jehu's companions no doubt wondered what had happened, but Jehu's immediate response was "You know the sort and how they babble!" (2 Kgs 9:11). Probably seeing the oil still on his head, Jehu's companions pressed him, and he revealed that he had been anointed king over Israel. Jehu set about immediately to wipe out the Omrid dynasty and at last brought an end to Jezebel's and Ahab's line in the north.

The activities of the prophetic bands were not limited to testifying to kings, however. It seems that most of the time they engaged in ecstatic worship around the boundaries of settled areas, preparing to be commanded by the Lord or by the head prophet to speak truth to power. As such, they formed an important reservoir of spiritual awareness during the period of the monarchy. There were several different bands (2 Kgs 2:3, 5, 15; 5:22) going back and forth between the wilderness and various cities to hear from God and then bring God's words to the people who were going about their daily routines. We know that they left their families in settled areas (2 Kgs 4:1–7) and lived communally in prophetic lodges (2 Kgs 6:1–7). They ate communal meals that were frequently presided over by the head prophet at the time (2 Kgs 4:38–44).

In short, the prophets lived weird/holy lives in order to be professional witnesses to God's visions. They drew special attention to the divergence between the ways of God and the actions of the kings. This is why the proverb "Is Saul also among the prophets?" retained such rhetorical power in Israel. Even though he was seized by a prophetic spirit on multiple occasions, the assumed answer to the question is no. Even David, a man after God's own heart who composed beautiful and haunting psalms to the Lord, was not a prophet but required the service of the prophet Nathan, among others, to correct him when he had gone astray.

Samuel, Elijah, and Elisha were all strongly connected with the prophetic bands, and many of their travels were centered around visiting the different prophetic troops and religious centers where they sought the Lord (1 Sam 7:16). Later prophets would reference this professional class of prophets to announce their ministry. God claimed superiority for Jeremiah over the professional prophetic troops by announcing that he was a prophet from before birth (Jer 1:5). On the other hand, Amos was emphatic that he had nothing to do with the pro-

> **The prophets lived weird/holy lives in order to be professional witnesses to God's visions.**

phetic bands (Amos 7:14). God has always spoken to whomever God wills, and membership in a prophetic band was not a prerequisite for hearing from the Lord. However, God seemed pleased to use semipermanent wilderness dwellers whose main job was to seek the Lord daily in community in order to bring a vision and message of correction from God to the leaders of God's people.

The organized prophetic bands lasted through at least part of the exilic experience (Ezra 5:2), but as the ruling structures changed during various occupations of the Holy Land, those with a prophetic vision seemed to have less access to speak directly to the powerful. The voices in the wilderness never died out entirely, however. Certainly by the time of the advent of the Messiah, God's people were once again hearing from God through prophets with wilderness visions.

Emulating the Lord

It is fitting that early in Jesus's ministry, he ventured out to the wilderness around Jordan (Matt 3:1) to be baptized by his relative. John was the prophetic fulfillment of Isaiah's words about God's voice in the wilderness (Isa 40:3). Jesus, and John before him, took up the mantle of the wilderness prophetic bands in going out to the unsettled places to hear from the Lord and then give testimony to the rulers and the powerful in the cities. John made it his mission to call the people to repentance and argue against the behavior of Herod Antipater with regard to his second wife. Just as Nathan had done centuries earlier, John spoke against a ruler of Israel marrying another man's wife. John faired quite a bit worse than Nathan, however, and was executed by Herod Antipater.

Shortly before he was killed, John had the honor of baptizing Jesus. It was at this time that both John (Gospels of Mark and John) and Jesus (Gospel of Matthew) saw heaven open and the Holy Spirit in the shape of a dove descend upon Jesus (Mark 1:10; John 1:32; and Matt 3:16). They heard the voice of God say, "This is / You are my Son, the Beloved, with whom / you I am well pleased" (combining Mark 1:11 and Matt 3:17). Truly, these men went to the wilderness, saw a vision, and heard from God. Just as in the days of old, God was visually moving and leading the people forward.

Jesus's baptism was far from the only time that he spent in the wilderness seeking direction from God. As Luke 5:15 points out, Jesus *often* withdrew to the wilderness to pray. Jesus sought "lonely places" outside of settled areas to speak with God. And since Jesus felt drawn to do this, we have in Jesus a model to emulate.

To be clear, Jesus had no problem praying around people, and he frequently attended synagogue services. But Jesus's preferred places to pray seem to have been the mountains. On his mountain prayer retreats, Jesus occasionally brought his disciples (Luke 9:29), but more often, the biblical text says that he went alone (e.g., Luke 6:12; Matt 14:23; and Mark 6:46).

God's people are warned throughout Scripture about the dangers of idolatrous "high places" of worship. Not demolishing these places was a major stain on the otherwise relatively well-approved reigns of the kings of Judah (e.g., 1 Kgs 15:14). But we see in the behavior of Jesus that just because places are high in elevation does not automatically disqualify them as places of worship and praise. If one goes to worship the Living God in spirit and in truth, the mountains can be a wonderful place for seeking to hear from the Lord.

The mountains were not the only place that Jesus sought to hear from God. After Jesus heard that John the Baptizer had been murdered by the state, he withdrew alone by boat to a solitary place (Matt 14:13), no doubt to pray to God about the execution of his beloved relative and the anguish about his own impending murder.

Aside from crisis, Jesus frequently made time to be alone with God. One of my favorite images from Scripture is from Mark 1:35: "Early in the morning, while it was still dark, he got up and slipped out to a solitary place to pray" (my translation). I am not sure why, but the idea of Jesus as an early riser, sneaking around the sleeping disciples, delights me. It probably appeals to my fondness for trying to sneak out of my sons' room after I put them down and sneaking out of my wife's and my bedroom so I can have a coffee and quiet time in the morning before anyone else wakes up.

Sometimes, however, Jesus's solitary places included his friends. One of Jesus's questions for the disciples is prefaced with "Once, while Jesus was praying alone, with his disciples" (Luke 9:18; my translation). Jesus and his disciples were probably alone together frequently. Certainly this was the case in Gethsemane, when Jesus felt terribly alone and betrayed by his sleeping disciples, who did not keep watch in prayer with him. Jesus's patterns are similar to the prophetic bands who lived communally in the wilderness places and sought the word of God.

The most important thing to remember about Jesus going out to the wilderness to pray is that it was not usually a long journey. Jesus ducked out of the routine of healing, teaching, and walking, usually in the morning. But he was back to his normal activities later in the day. Jesus went to nearby geographic features where he could be alone, or alone with his friends, but the wildernesses that Jesus entered were more about holy *time* than holy *space*. Jesus made time to pray and to seek to hear from God without ceasing to live his life or conduct his ministry. Even in the midst of our modern cities, we can find places and times that afford us moments alone with God. That is what Jesus was doing when he went to the wilderness places.

Going to the wilderness to pray and seek a vision of God's guidance was an important part of the earthly life of Jesus of Nazareth. Insofar as we seek to be conformed to his image (Rom 8:29), we would do well to imitate his regular withdrawal to "lonely places." But how does one arrive at wilderness places to hear God? One possible way to emulate Jesus is to go on a modern quest to a weird/holy place to hear from God.

> **Jesus made time to pray and to seek to hear from God.**

Catching a Vision: Modern Wilderness Experiences

Adjusting to the first few years of my marriage was particularly difficult. Both my wife and I were in our thirties when we finally married after almost seven years of dating. We love each other deeply, but we were used to living by ourselves. Moving in together after we got married required both of us to make changes, which we were both slow to do. And like every married couple, we disagreed about money issues. We also began the work of sorting through how we wanted the other to express and reciprocate emotions and intimacy. I moved from where I had been living, studying, and teaching for the years prior to where she had been living for the previous nine years. I was entering her life, habits, spaces, and customs in a way that she was not entering mine.

I was frequently by myself in a city that I knew pretty well, but it was not home yet. I knew several people, but most of them had day jobs and not available for friendly hangouts during the day when I took lengthy "breaks" from my dissertation writing. So I walked. I walked all over Columbus, Ohio. Just as I had covered twenty to thirty miles a day in the Sahara, so I covered at least that much ground walking around the city. Walking was helpful, just to be outside and active. But what was most helpful to me was being able to go someplace I had not been before, where there were no other people around, and think and pray. I found a few wilderness places and times in the city.

Columbus, like most midsized cities, has places right in the middle of it where most people do not go. The edges of rivers, under bridges, inside of railway tunnels, the edges of drainage ponds on the side of big box store parking lots, even off the trail in forested parks—in all of these places in an urban environment, one can be out of sight of the settled, ordinary areas. Jonathan Wilson-Hartgrove and the "New Monastics" movement call these the abandoned places of empire.[3] It is usually in these types of places that the folks who have opted out or been squeezed out of ordinary society cluster. Sarah, much more so than me, loves to make friends with people who are experiencing homelessness and live under bridges. I eventually benefited from some of those friendships. More often, though, I was looking to be alone with my thoughts and with God.

The best thinking that I ever did in these times—and I am convinced that these thoughts were a gift from God and not any particular brilliance from me—was simply to ask God what was best and where God was moving. Daily, I felt annoyed, lonely, and stressed, and I did not see that getting any better through my own actions. God took me out of familiar places and away from the distractions of comforting food and diverting drink to wilderness places in order to help me focus on where God was leading me: dying to self and submitting to my spouse in humble service. That journey is certainly easier plotted out than it was/is actually walked out.

Self-sacrifice and loving service to others came up again and again as I read Scriptures about Jesus.

The first step of a wilderness journey that I would advise others to take is to literally step away from the places where you have been. Go someplace close to your house or apartment that is new, uncommon, or even uncomfortable—but not unsafe! And once you are in the wilderness, be like the Israelites and look to God for your orientation. For me, it was not even a process of audibly hearing God's voice or even feeling led in prayer. I just read Scripture about love and Jesus. Self-sacrifice and loving service to others came up again and again as I read Scriptures about Jesus.

There are, of course, many ways to look to God for orientation in the wilderness. The counsel of godly friends or hearing from God directly may be the means of guidance that God gives you. Like the Israelite camp in the wilderness, it may be that you are not called to journey in a new direction and that God's message is for you to simply rest from your journey for a time. In any case, looking to God to see where God may be leading is the crucial first step of a blessed wilderness journey.

133

Along the way, there can be temptations and traps. Just as Balaam tempted the Israelites in the wilderness, so we also can face temptation. All too often, I would rather be right than holy. But this is not the wilderness journey to which God has called me. I should not fall into the sin of Balaam—that is, being jealous, prideful, and resentful. Again, everyone's journey in the wilderness places of our lives looks different. Here, however, is some beneficial one-size-fits-all guidance: utilize a brief physical journey to a place beyond normal your routine to lessen the desire to have what others have, to be prideful in what you have, and to wish that others should suffer.

At least for me, it is important to try to bring as few gadgets and entertainment sources as possible, to get away from all the *stuff* that distracts my heart and attention from God and from those I should be loving. It is only when I am someplace remote from my normal life that I can catch a vision of the life that God wants *me* to be living without thinking of what others may be doing that irritates me. The trick, then, is to retain that vision while returning to my normal, everyday life.

I want to pause right here and state for the record, in case it has not been clear yet, that I am not good at this stuff. I feel like God has impressed upon me repeatedly the value of gentle service for others and not desiring more than I have been given (which is already a lot, in any case). I acknowledge seeing that vision from God of a holy and blessed life. And yet every day is a struggle. Still, every night before I go to sleep (well, if I don't fall asleep while I'm putting down my sons), I pray that God would help me be tender toward my family and lovingly sacrifice myself for them.

My prayers at night do not always turn into actions in the morning. But I want them to. I urgently desire to humbly serve my wife better. When she asked if I would paint her toenails this morning, I initially refused. She had just used nail polish remover, which is my second most hated smell. I can smell the stuff for days, and it honestly makes me want to stop breathing. But after I calmed down, I agreed to paint her toenails after all. And I did a pretty good job too. A few hours ago, I received a text that said, "Go writer-hunk, go! Thanks for painting my toenails, they look great [heart]!" So today was a somewhat rare win in the long battle to be a little humbler in my marriage and family life.

The action point here is simply to think and pray at night or in the morning for a vision of a small sacrifice that you could do to serve someone else. Or even more basic, maybe you could pray to have a more meek or humble disposition. What would it look like to scale back the effort of trying to win? If those whom Jesus welcomes into the kingdom of heaven are good and faithful *servants*, how can we strive each day to be a little more servant-like? That said, I want to acknowledge that submission, meekness, and service are things that I, as a cis-het, able-bodied white man with letters before and after my name and with incredible amounts of power and privilege, need to work on. God may be calling you to something else.

My last bit of advice for having a vision of what God might be doing is to seek out the voices of prophets in the wilderness. Just as biblical prophets, John the Baptizer, and Jesus critiqued the sins of leaders that trickled down into society, so we ought to be willing to hear and act on the words of God coming out of the mouths of prophetic speakers today. People of good faith can have differences of opinion on which prophetic voices to focus on, and that is OK. We are a body of Christ with many different parts and different roles, and we can be concerned about different issues.

For me personally, I value the voices of D. L. Mayfield, Rabbi Abraham Joshua Heschel, Dr. Cornel West, and Shane Claiborne, among others, for their calls to active repentance from violent empire building and expansion. You may find those voices also point you to what God is doing. There are many prophetic voices out there, and I advise you to listen to them. Be blessed in tuning in to the vision of what God calls you to do *and in doing it*. Be aware also that the biblical prophets were often persecuted and driven into the wilderness by those they sought to reorient toward God's vision of love and holiness. In the same way, modern-day prophets may be persecuted by the powers that they attempt to speak truth to.

The wilderness is a holy place because it is not part of our regular routine, and because it is not "home" for anyone, it is weird. That is its defining characteristic. When we don't feel at home in the wilderness, we are less complacent and absorbed in the normal. It is precisely into this holy weirdness that God chooses to speak and even appear occasionally. But when God appeared to the Israelites, let Balaam "see," or even spoke through the prophets, the revelation of a vision in the wilderness was not a goal unto itself. Rather, God was pronouncing that a marginal group of Israelite ex-slaves and defecting Egyptians (Exod 12:38) was particularly beloved of God and would figure prominently in God's actions on earth. In the next chapter, we turn to how God pays particular attention to women in their wilderness moments and pronounces them beloved prophets, community members, and champions of justice.

GUIDED REFLECTIONS

1. Returning to Rashi's idea of God "taking" the human and putting it in the garden of Eden as a kind of holy seduction, if God were trying to entice you to go someplace or do something, where/what would it be? Spend some time thinking about what things might be a blessing to God (and possibly you) but that God would have to entice you to do.

2. When in your life have you clearly heard from God or seen a vision of what God wanted you to do? What was the situation of your life at that time? Were you in some kind of wilderness? Where did God lead you? How do you keep this call alive in your life to walk in obedience to what God wants for you?

3. Think about times in your life when you have simply felt the intimacy of God's presence. What were those experiences like? What did they teach you?

4. How can we be certain that we are truly seeing with eyes uncovered? How does our culture, and especially our church or religious culture, sometimes act as blinders to prevent us from seeing what God is doing

in the larger body of Christ or even in the wider world? It is so difficult to interrogate our own culture. How would a fish describe water? It has no concept of "wet" because it has no concept of "dry." The best advice that I can offer is to have conversations with others outside of your own religious community/denomination. Where do they see the spirit of God moving? How does their analysis help you think? How can we be like Peter in Acts 10, who, after speaking with a gentile God-fearer, learns a bit more of what God is up to in the world (Acts 10:34)?

5. How can we seek to be humble, meek, and generous in our everyday lives?

6. Who are some prophetic voices that you hear in the world today? How is their message similar to or different from the prophetic critique of the power and faithlessness of Israelite and Judahite kings? For another exercise, spend time reading one or all of the following passages: Isaiah 6–10; Matthew 5–7; and/or Matthew 20–25. How would you summarize the key messages in these texts? How are they useful prophetic guidance for today?

7. How will you go about entering into the wilderness to catch a vision from/of God? Identify some action steps.

4

Women in the Wilderness

Then the prophet Miriam, Aaron's sister, took a tambourine
in her hand; and all the women went out after her with
tambourines and with dancing.

—Exodus 15:20

Or when a spirit of jealousy comes on a man and he is jealous
of his wife; then he shall set the woman before the Lord,
and the priest shall apply this entire law to her.

—Numbers 5:30

Katherine Doob Sakenfeld wrote that, like the Israelite women in
the book of Numbers, those who engage in feminist Bible studies and feminist readings of Scripture are also "in the wilderness,
awaiting the land."[1] She meant that feminist scholarship departs
from the security of the established, androcentric scholarship of
the academy in order to look, and hope, for "not just a space, but
for a place within the scholarly community and within the church, a
hope not yet fully realized."[2] Sakenfeld wrote those words over thirty

years ago, but not enough has changed for them to no longer apply. Gender-sensitive readings of Scripture can be, at the same time, profoundly unsettling and profoundly healing. This chapter invites you to step into a wilderness experience with women of Scripture, who faced up to patriarchy and pushed back. It is helpful for me, and us, to return to their stories again and again until we learn the lessons they are trying to teach us in our own wilderness times.

There and Back Again

Like the title of Bilbo Baggins's memoirs, *There and Back Again*, my relationship with the wilderness has a cyclical pattern. During the periods of normal, boring life, I long for adventure. Waking up with my son at five o'clock in the

> I prefer to learn from those who have gone before.

morning and finally having that last conversation with my wife around eleven o'clock at night and doing the same thing every day (my son doesn't quite understand the concept of weekends yet) grows tiresome. I miss the days of getting in the car in the States or hopping a train in Morocco and just going on an adventure into the wilderness—somewhere new, holy, and weird. But when I am on even the shortest of business trips or in a new, uncomfortable situation, I miss my family pretty quickly and can't wait to get home to them.

It is not always our desires for adventure that take us out of our comfort zone into an unsettled life. My mother-in-law, Kathy, did not ask to be placed in an ethical quandary as to how she should act in the political wilderness. She was—and really, we are all still—lost in unfamiliar territory. Many people respond by looking to themselves, finding what is important, and moving on, holding that as central. That may work well. The historian in me is uncomfortable with that approach, though, because looking to what is important to the individual, or even to the small in-group, frequently and quickly leads us to disregard or devalue what is important and life-giving for the larger community. I prefer to learn from those who have gone before, who have faced the wilderness and emerged, changed and gnarly but with a story to tell and a blessing to share with their community.

In Defense of Miriam

If there was ever someone who was gnarled and changed by the wilderness but nevertheless had a story to tell and blessings for her community, it was the prophet Miriam. Miriam was one of the five women who saved Israelite children, including Moses, at the beginning of the Exodus story: Shiphrah, Puah, Jochebed, Miriam, and Batya (Pharaoh's daughter). She watched over her infant brother in the reeds and then bravely approached the daughter of Pharaoh with a plan to reunite her mother and brother (Exod 2:7–8). When Miriam grew up, she led Israelites in praise and worship at the crossing of the sea and the destruction of the pursuing Egyptian army (Exod 15:20). She was a leader in the Israelite camp and was recognized as such. Even in the book of Chronicles, which provides an almost exclusively androcentric genealogy, Miriam is mentioned along with Aaron and Moses (1 Chr 6:3).

Yet for all her acclaim and importance to the children of Israel, Miriam, the eldest of Amram and Jochebed's children, frequently gets a bad rap. This is not completely without reason. Miriam led her brother Aaron in complaining about Moses. We know this because the verb form of "spoke" used in the following passage is singular feminine, suggesting that it was really Miriam who spoke against Moses rather than Miriam *and* Aaron. And the punishment is leveled against Miriam only rather than against Aaron:

> Miriam and Aaron spoke against Moses because of the Cushite woman whom he had married (for he had indeed married a Cushite woman); and they said, "Has the Lord spoken only through Moses? Has he not spoken through us also?" And the Lord heard it. . . . Suddenly the Lord said to Moses, Aaron, and Miriam, "Come out, you three, to the tent of meeting." So the three of them came out . . .
>
> And the anger of the Lord was kindled against them, and he departed.
>
> When the cloud went away from over the tent, Miriam had become leprous, as white as snow. . . . But the Lord said to Moses, "If her father had but spit in her face, would she not bear her shame for seven days? Let her be shut out of the camp for seven days, and after that she may be brought in again." So Miriam was shut out of the camp for seven days; and the people did not set out on the march until Miriam had been brought in again. (Num 12:1–2, 4, 9–10, 14–15)

This passage elicits a wealth of commentary from the rabbis because many strange details are included. The first of which is that Miriam's punishment serves as an occasion for expressing how dearly loved she is, as well as demonstrating her public discipline. Aaron and even Moses, whom she complained against, were quick to intercede for their sister in desperate terms.

In addition to Moses and Aaron, the entire camp of the Israelites waited for Miriam to be ritually clean before moving on. Think of it: over six hundred thousand men of military age, their extended families, the Levites, the priests, and the holy articles all waited for Miriam to be welcomed into the camp again before they moved (M *Sotah* 1:9). For all the other people who suffered leprosy or skin issues and had to be relocated outside of the camp, the movement of the Israelites did not stop. They had to catch up on their own, though it would be surprising if such a massive camp moved very quickly. We are told explicitly that the people refused to go on without Miriam. This is said for no one else.

Even God uses the punishment of Miriam as an occasion to also declare her special position. This is one of the first instances in the biblical text of God addressing an individual as God's child. In answering Moses's and Aaron's prayers on behalf of Miriam, God asked if her father had spit in her face, would not she be shamed for seven days? God was saying what had been done to Miriam was like a father dishonoring his daughter. It is a backhanded compliment, but it is a claim of parentage nonetheless. God said that Miriam should be regarded as if her father (God) had dishonored her. She was to be in isolation for seven days but then welcomed back into the camp as God's daughter (*Sifrei* on

Numbers, 106; *Sifrei Zuta* 12:14–15). If this sounds like the rabbis are stretching the case, please consider the legal issues at stake and how God mitigates them.

According to Leviticus 13, the normal procedure for someone who has a skin issue (like leprosy) is for them to be brought to a priest to be inspected. Then the person would have been isolated outside the camp for seven days. After that week, the priest would inspect the person again. If the situation remained the same or improved, the person was isolated another seven days and, upon another positive inspection by a priest, was welcomed back into the camp. If the second inspection went badly, however, that person was declared leprous and permanently unclean unless in the case of a miraculous healing or the entire body turning white. The minimum period of time spent outside the camp, according to the law that God had just given to Moses was fourteen days, with priestly verification that the leprosy was not spreading. Miriam, however, only spent seven days outside the camp and was pronounced able to return after that period. Therefore, at the very same time that God punished Miriam, God also acted as her priest to pronounce her clean and ready to return after a week.

Miriam was indeed punished, but God acted peculiarly in this case. When Kohath and the Reubenites made a seemingly similar claim to be equal to Moses, they were annihilated from the face of the earth. Moses was furious with them. But when Miriam and Aaron spoke to Moses, the text does not describe Moses's anger at Miriam at all. On the contrary, he immediately prayed for her. The rabbis imagine Moses drawing a circle on the ground and petulantly declaring to God, "I will not come out of this circle to lead your people until you heal my sister Miriam" (*Avot de-Rabbi Nathan*, ver. A, 9). Miriam's punishment was only to have white skin for a week. But she was spoken of as God's own daughter, God acted as her priest to welcome her back to the camp, Moses interceded for her, and the entire Israelite assembly waited for her before moving on. Why this difference in treatment from others who spoke against Moses?

Miriam did not overstep her authority or claim a role that was not hers already. Miriam was a leader of the Israelites along with her brothers. God spoke through the prophet Micah, saying, "I brought you up out of Egypt, and redeemed you from the land of slavery. I sent Moses to lead you, also Aaron and Miriam" (Mic 6:4 NIV). In Exodus 15:20, Miriam is explicitly called a prophet. She was one of the seven key women prophets of Israel: Sarah, Miriam, Deborah, Hannah, Abigail, Huldah, and Hadassah/Esther. That she was called a prophet before she took up drums and voice to perform the song of the sea begs an obvious question: How did she earn the distinction of a prophet? That is, where/when/what did she prophesy? The rabbis have an answer for this question that nicely ties up loose ends in Numbers. Exodus 2 says,

> Now a man from the house of Levi went and married a Levite woman. The woman conceived and bore a son; and when she saw that he was a fine baby, she hid him for three months. When she could hide him no longer she got a papyrus basket for him, and plastered it with bitumen and pitch; she put the child in it and placed it among the reeds on the bank of the river. His sister stood at a distance, to see what would happen to him (Exod 2:1–4).

Amram and Jochebed married and then gave birth to Moses. But the baby Moses already had an older sister who was able to stand at a distance and watch. This seems strange. Not wanting to imagine that the prophet Miriam and the high priest Aaron were born out of wedlock, the rabbis argued that when Amram heard the news that Pharaoh wished to murder the Israelite boy babies, he decided that he would never risk having to watch a future son of his be killed. He already had a daughter, Miriam, and a son, Aaron. Amram was satisfied that his name would live on through his children. So he divorced his wife Jochebed and advocated that the other Israelites do the same to prevent their children from being killed.

But then Miriam came and prophesied to her own father, "What you have done is twice as evil as what pharaoh has done. For he sought only to kill the boys, but you have prevented boys and girls from being born. Relent and re-marry your wife, and our savior will be born to you" (BT *Sotah* 12b). Amram saw the wisdom in her counsel and (re)married Jochebed, and she gave birth to a(nother) son, Moses. Thus Miriam became known as a prophet and was especially known as a prophet who advised spouses to return to each other after a period of separation. Scholars argue that this is what she was doing with Moses when she spoke up about his wife.[3]

> **Miriam became known as a prophet.**

Twice in Scripture it has been noted that Moses was working too hard and not sharing the workload of leadership of the Israelites. Jethro in Exodus 18 and God in Numbers 11 both helped

Moses share the responsibility of leadership of the people. Moses, like many leaders, tended to take on too much and neglected his family. Especially when Moses was at his breaking point in Numbers 11, an arrangement was made for him to share his leadership role with other elders. It is very lonely at the top, even with helpers, and Moses was focused on doing the work of the Lord on behalf of God's people. He did not, in other words, have time for marital relations with his wife Zipporah.

Moses had already sent his wife and sons away once (Exod 18:2). Even when his father-in-law brought his sons and wife to him, the biblical account only carries the details of his warm reuniting with Jethro, saying nothing about Moses's marital family. Immediately Moses began telling Jethro stories about what God had done, and then they had a meal with Aaron and the elders of the Israelites. The next day, Moses was back judging the Israelites without any note about his wife and children. To make matters worse, before the giving of the commandments on Sinai, God told all the Israelites to refrain from sexual relations for three days before the beginning of the revelation of the law (Exod 19:15). Recalling the next events years later, Moses remembered God telling him after the beginning of the revelation of God's law, "Go say to [the Israelites], 'Return to your tents.' But you, stand here by me" (Deut 5:30–31). The Israelites were able to go "back to their tents," a euphemism for returning to their family life and normal sexual activity. But Moses was to stay with the Lord, in celibacy. And so Zipporah was deprived of her marital rights (BT *Shabbat* 87a).

Considering all this, Miriam's words of complaint take on a whole new meaning: "Miriam and Aaron spoke against Moses because of the Cushite[4] woman whom he had married (for he had indeed married a Cushite woman); and they said, 'Has the Lord indeed spoken only through Moses? Has he not spoken through us as well?'" (Num 12:1–2). Miriam—and remember the verb "spoke" indicates it was only Miriam—was speaking against Moses not because she did not like his Cushite/Midianite wife but because Moses was not loving her well enough, in Miriam's opinion.

Remember, Miriam was regarded as a prophet specifically for her role in rekindling the marital and sexual relations between her own parents—and all the Israelites—after they separated. She was just being true to form and doing the same thing between Moses and Zipporah. However, even a prophetess does not get to go against the will of the Lord without consequences. Marriage is important, especially in the community of God's people, as in it, many, though certainly not all, are called to practice humility, mercy, and grace. But marriage is not the only, or even necessarily the best, station in life (1 Cor 7:8; Matt 19:10–12), and in advocating for Moses to shift his attention from an exclusive focus on the Lord to Zipporah, the rabbis understood that Miriam ran afoul of God.

As a result of her well-meaning but rejected offer to share Moses's leadership burden so that he could reunite sexually with Zipporah, Miriam was censured publicly with leprous white skin. But Miriam was also honored publicly by being spoken of as God's daughter (albeit like a daughter who was spit upon), and God personally performed the service of a Levitical priest for her. It was her concern for Moses's marriage to Zipporah and lack of ambition to grasp a role that was not already hers that led to her punishment being so wildly divergent from that of Korah. He had said roughly the same words, but in a very different spirit and with very different consequences.

Miriam had always been and continued to be a prophet whose heart was dedicated to loving God and preserving relationships with and among her people. Her leadership and advocating for inclusion and embrace of foreigners stands as a model for us in wilderness moments in our own individual and collective lives. If we stand up for those who are cast aside or forgotten, will we not also be a source of refreshment[5] to our communities, like Miriam? When life becomes unsettled, it is more necessary than ever to follow the example of the prophet Miriam: to look for opportunities to offer praise and thanksgiving to God, to seize opportunities to mend ruptures in our communities, and to advocate for women's rightful place in all levels of leadership.

Returning to the Wilderness with Zelophehad's Daughters

Like the Israelites, we are not led to the wilderness as individuals or as the body of Christ just once. Rather, we need to renew our relationship with the holy weirdness to which we have been called. Frequently, we need to return to the wilderness to relearn a lesson or continue with progress that has stalled. As an example, we as a community are still figuring out what it means for there to be neither male nor female in Christ (Gal 3:28). Several Christian denominations and/or individual congregations still block women from full service. The hope of equality and then lack of fulfillment of this hope is a theme in the book of Numbers.

A man named Zelophehad from the tribe of Manasseh died having five daughters and no sons (Num 26:33). Crucially, in a section that focuses on preserving names, the women in question are named here as Mahlah, Tirzah, Hoglah, Milcah, and Noah. In the next chapter, the five women address the Israelite community with a concern, among other things, about their father's name not being preserved. Since Zelophehad had died without sons, he would have no allotment of land in the upcoming conquest (Num 26:52–56). Prior to this time, among the Israelites, there was no provision for women inheriting from their father. The five women stood before Moses, Eleazar the priest, all the elders, the whole community, and the Lord at the tent of meeting and demanded that they, too, receive land along with their uncles (Num 27:2–4). This was incredibly brave. The last time a woman stood at the entrance to the tent of meeting and attempted to change the status quo, Miriam's skin was turned white.

In this case, God's response was that the daughters of Zelophehad were correct. They had challenged what God had just said through Moses about inheritance in the land, in addition to patriarchal notions about ownership of not just goods but land. God declared, in a literal translation of the Hebrew, "Yes [to what the] daughters of Zelophehad say" (Num 27:7). Their father's inheritance should be passed to them and their names should be equal to those of their uncles and male relatives in having an ancestral plot of land assigned to each of them in the tribal allotments of Manasseh. Seeking to preserve the name of their father and to prevent themselves from becoming destitute or being forced to marry to have any resources, the women challenged Moses and God's previous instruction and were declared to be correct in their demand for justice. Not only were Mahlah, Tirzah, Hoglah, Milcah, and Noah granted justice, but their challenge of the patriarchy led to the promulgation of a new law that women in subsequent generations could inherit property from their fathers, albeit only in the same situation in which the father had no sons (Num 27:8).

And yet nine chapters later, the men of Zelophehad's clan returned to Moses. Cynically, they appear just before Moses and male leaders, not before the priests or the whole congregation, and not at the tent of meeting as Zelophehad's daughters had done (Num 36:1). Already, the careful reader knows that all the Israelite women, including Mahlah, Tirzah, Hoglah, Milcah, and Noah, have been excluded from the meeting. The men told Moses that if Zelophehad's daughters were allowed to marry whomever they wanted outside the tribe, then "their fathers'" land would be taken away from them and incorporated into the tribes into which the women married. Even the Jubilee Year would not return the holdings to Manasseh (Num 36:4). Unlike Mahlah, Tirzah, Hoglah, Milcah, and Noah, their uncles proposed not a solution but rather a problem.[6] This time, rather than reporting the speech of God directly, the biblical text only presents Moses speaking on behalf of the mouth of the Lord, saying that the uncles' concern is valid (Num 36:5). The daughters of Zelophehad may marry whomever they want to, but their spouses must come from the tribe of their father. Like the earlier instance, this particular issue concerning

Zelophehad's daughters also generated a legal standard that whenever Israelite women came to possess real estate, they must marry within their ancestral tribe. The rights of Israelite women to inherit and marry whomever they pleased were constrained because of men's fear after the initial provision from the Lord offered inheritance equality (if not equity) for Mahlah, Tirzah, Hoglah, Milcah, and Noah.

This provision and then retraction of women's rights is a sad, ongoing reality in the patriarchal world. But it also points in a hopeful direction in which women successfully challenge androcentric legal codes and are declared right by God. Further, reading this story helps give us insights into Israelite society:

> Reading a text as it stands may even help us discover a historical reality (not just an authorial reality) that we had heretofore supposed to be nonexistent. What if ancient Israel really believed that God did not want women [like Mahlah, Tirzah, Hoglah, Milcah, and Noah] to be subordinated to men? . . . What if women prophets [like Miriam] were quite ordinary?[7]

Scripture points out here that women in the wilderness camp were at least able to appear before religious/political power and argue their own case (e.g., 1 Kgs 3:16–28), inherit not just property but land, have tribal land assigned to their names on par with their male relatives, and choose their own spouses, even when drastically limited through patriarchal conniving (Num 36:6). It is necessary for us to return to the wilderness experiences of women to fight for and preserve helpful interpretations that foreground these freedoms that have been denied women for centuries. Phyllis Trible describes this struggle to promote and defend life-giving readings of Scripture:

> Jacob's defiant words to the stranger I take as a challenge to the Bible itself: "I will not let you go unless you bless me." I will not let go of the book unless it blesses me. I will struggle with it. I will not turn it over to my enemies that it curse me. Neither will I turn it over to friends who wish to curse it.[8]

We need to return to Scripture continually to struggle with it, to extract that which is a blessing for ourselves and for others, and to resist ways that harmful interpretations can hurt ourselves and others. The story of Mahlah, Tirzah, Hoglah, Milcah, and Noah can—and, I argue, should—be read as combating the patriarchal dehumanization of women by preserving women's names among the other tribal land recipients and describing their freedoms in ancient Israel. But if reading the story of Zelophehad's daughters as a liberating text that preserves and potentially expands rights for women is difficult, seeing Numbers 5 as a blessing for women trapped in a dangerous situation has proven almost entirely elusive for Christians until recently.

Rebuking a Spirit of Jealousy

The ritual in Numbers 5:11–31 for determining a wife's guilt when her husband is overcome with jealousy has been troubling interpreters for thousands of years. The test only exists for women. Wives who are overcome by a spirit of jealousy and suspect their husbands have other sexual partners have no recourse to a similar test for their husbands.[9] The tradition in the biblical text makes a public spectacle out of the accused woman, and the Mishnaic instructions for carrying out the ritual, recorded several hundreds of years later, are downright barbaric. But recent scholarship has pushed back on the negative view of this ritual, and some scholars, to be referenced below, view the ritual as liberative for women caught in a patriarchal system of accusation and with the inability to prove their innocence. But what was the actual ritual?

The biblical text prescribes the *Sotah* (a term for a woman suspected of adultery) ritual in three cases: (1) when a wife has had sex with a man other than her husband, but no one else knows and there are no witnesses (Num 5:12–13); (2) when a spirit of jealousy (*ruach qinah*) comes over a husband who has a wife who has had sex with another partner (Num 5:14); and (3) when a spirit of jealousy comes over a husband whose wife has *not* had sex with any other partners (Num 5:14). The man is not allowed to punish her himself, and she cannot be brought before a court or a judge because there are no witnesses against her. The husband's only way to find out for certain whether his wife was unfaithful to him was to bring his wife to the priest. The husband is instructed to bring an offering of unperfumed barley flour that would cause *his* sin of jealousy to be remembered—not forgotten (Num 5:15, 18, 25). The wife then presents the offering before the Lord on her husband's behalf (Num 5:18). The priest uncovers and possibly dishevels the wife's hair and has her stand before the altar at the tabernacle. The priest then takes holy water, presumably from the same source that the priests used to purify themselves (Exod 30:17–21), and fills a container. The priest adds dust from around the base of the altar. Finally, the priest writes on a scroll what can only be called an incantation formula and then washes it off into the water. The woman is asked to say "Amen" twice to agree to potential cursing and potential exoneration written by the ink, which now is part of the concoction. Then she drinks the holy water mixed with holy dust and holy words. If the woman has indeed committed adultery, parts of her body that are involved in sex and reproduction (though scholars differ on how to translate specific terms) will undergo massive, painful transformations that will confirm her guilt. If nothing happens, God will have confirmed her innocence. In the case of either outcome, her husband will be freed from guilt (by his sacrifice for jealousy).

Such a one-sided ritual in which a man can present his wife for this public ritual, proclaiming that he does not trust her, may fairly be called a "text of terror" along with other horrifying passages of maltreatment of humans in the Bible.[10] Yet this ritual, read correctly, is full of reversal and parody.[11] The husband is suspect if he accuses his wife without witnesses, and it is his sin that requires an offering. The Sotah ritual is seen, by the husband, as a sort of antidote to public suspicion of male fragility and fear of women's threatening sexuality, but in cases when the wife is exonerated (more on the frequency of the ritual uncovering secret adultery below), the husband's irrational jealousy and fear of his wife's sexuality are confirmed.[12]

In the Sotah ritual, the wife consumes the holiest dust available in ancient Israel and literally drinks the name of God after presenting an offering on her husband's behalf. In her attempt to see the Sotah ritual's positive outcomes for women, scholar Alice Bach points out that the Sotah ritual is the only trial by ordeal in the Hebrew Bible.[13] This is significant because, in a legal system in which guilt is established only by multiple witnesses (Deut 19:15; Num 35:30), God designed a process where, in the absence of witnesses able to exonerate a woman from charges of adultery (or convict her), God acts as a witness on behalf of innocent women to end suspicion against her.

Further, the ritual was designed to preclude accidental false positives. The holiest dust from the foot of the altar would not have embittered the waters.[14] Israel and Egypt produced a potentially poisonous ink (BT *Megillah* 1:2) that could have ensured that whoever drank the incantation that was washed into the waters would become ill. But the Sotah ritual called for an expensive, harmless (and potentially tasty) mix of soot, gum arabia, and water (BT *Sotah* 2:4).[15] Thus the "waters of bitterness/cursing" were really waters of blessing that allowed a woman to vindicate herself from a false accusation.[16] The waters of the Sotah ritual, rather than harming innocent women, act as holy water that drives out a spirit of jealousy from suspicious husbands by ridiculing them for their sinful jealousy and fear of their wives' sexuality. Even if the ritual worked out badly for the accused woman, she was not killed, as was the normal punishment for adultery.[17] Her punishment was that she could no longer conceive children, not that she would die. God is *never* a capital witness against women accused of adultery (John 20:1–18).

As the rabbis dealt with this passage from the Israelites' wilderness experience, they fell into decidedly two camps—those who viewed it as liberation for women accused falsely and those who read the ritual instructions as a way to weed out all the secret illicit sex that they feared was happening all around them. Some of the instructions—from the Mishnah, for instance—are particularly violent and humiliating to the accused woman. They involved insulting her, tearing up her clothes, and displaying her partially nude. The Mishnaic account instructed the priest to dishevel her hair such that, even though she was not caught in the act of adultery and there were no witnesses against her, she looked as if she had been caught in flagrante delicto (M *Sotah* 1:5–6). I have often wondered if it was the misogyny of certain rabbis (though obviously not all) who did not wish to see jealous husbands embarrassed by exonerated wives that caused them to add such dehumanization and embarrassment to a ritual that was apparently designed to be liberating for women. A later rabbinic writing from the school of thought that viewed the Sotah ritual as designed to prove unfairly accused women innocent repudiates these added, cruel embarrassments from the Mishnah, saying, "It is not appropriate to degrade the Israelite daughters in a manner that exceeds what is written in the scripture" (*Sifre*, Numbers 11).

Yet even as the Mishnah added insult to injury, the same document points out that the Sotah ritual was something that women *wanted and chose* to undergo to establish their innocence. The Mishnah points out that even after a husband presented an accused wife to the priests, the wife could choose not to go through with the ritual if she did not want to drink (M *Sotah* 1:3). The accused wife could admit that she had had illicit sex, or she could refuse to drink without admitting guilt (M *Sotah* 3:3). In either case, if the wife chose not to drink, with or without admitting guilt, she was not stoned for adultery but merely had to divorce her husband and forfeit the marital good stipulated to her in their wedding contract (M *Sotah* 1:5). Instant divorce seems like a good solution to get away from a man who was willing to submit his wife to public ridicule and a potentially deadly ordeal because he suspected her without proof or witnesses. Women chose to undergo the ritual, though, even after the priest was ordered to beg the woman not to go through with it (M *Sotah* 1:4).

The rabbinic commentary on the ritual from Numbers goes on to point out how the Sotah ritual was mystically egalitarian. While the waters searched the woman's body for hints of adultery, the rabbis say that the waters also searched "him" (M *Sotah* 5:1). This "him" may be the woman's illicit paramour, if there was one, but more likely, it was the husband himself who brought his wife for the ritual. The wife has some manner of reversal, in drinking the waters, that the rabbis say also searched her husband for his potential adultery. The Sotah ritual was eventually stopped because rabbis decided it was not fair to have women undergo a one-sided ordeal while so many men were committing adultery: "When adulterers multiplied, the ceremony of the bitter waters ceased and it was Rabban Yohanan ben Zakkai who discontinued it, as it is said, 'I will not punish their daughters for fornicating, nor their daughters-in-law for committing adultery, for they themselves [commit illicit sex acts (a reference to Hos 4:14)]'" (M *Sotah* 9:9). Even before they ended the ritual, many rabbis were confused as to why almost no women were being convicted. These rabbis wondered if perhaps the wives' merit in other areas of their lives forestalled the effects (M *Sotah* 3:5). But other rabbis pushed back and said that this guesswork about why the Sotah ritual did not convict women impugned all the women that God had declared innocent (M *Sotah* 3:6).

So why was this ritual that gave women the ability to be declared by God as innocent of their husbands' spirit of jealousy given to the Israelites in the wilderness? Moses had set up law courts, but they were only to act on evidence brought forward by witnesses. The very definition of the Sotah issue is that there are no witnesses and that the man is overcome by a (evil) spirit of jealousy, for which he presents a sin offering. In the disorienting and confusing wilderness places in our lives, it can be easy to lash out at others, to blame our partners and friends for not understanding what we are going through. But the solution is not to unfairly accuse others, especially others who do not have the ability to defend themselves or prove their innocence. God stepped into the wilderness and said, in effect, "I will make an exception to my human witness-based legal system in just this one instance. I will act as a witness on behalf of or against accused women. In no case, guilt or innocence, will they face the normal punishment for adultery."

A close reading of the biblical text suggests that the ritual is designed to shame husbands for being jealous of their wives, who were almost never convicted. The rabbinic accounts point to a ritual that a woman undergoes only if she wants to prove her innocence beyond a doubt, which was almost always what happened. The implication for us, in our wilderness places, is to resist jealousy, not put up with false or unsupported accusations, and above all, believe the women.

Refuting Cozbi

It is worth mentioning the ways in which the women mentioned above all provide a counterexample of faithfulness to the duplicitous example of Cozbi the Midianite from Numbers 24. If any women from the book of Numbers are mentioned in churches, typically it would be Cozbi and her death at the hands of Phinehas. Yet the wilderness journeys offer several accounts of women as faithful and praiseworthy community members, frequently refuting the ways that Cozbi sought to undermine Israelite faithfulness.

Remember that Cozbi the Midianite had caused a *qubbah*, or ritual tent shrine, to be set up directly next to the dwelling of Zimri and his family. In this *qubbah*, sex would lead purposefully and directly to the worship of Baal of Peor. Contrary to how Cozbi sought to lead the Israelites into idolatrous worship of a foreign god by using seduction, Miriam sought to lead the Israelites in faithful worship of the God of Israel, who had just saved them from the Egyptians and the sea. Miriam also led the Israelites by appealing to their senses, but instead of orgies, she led through music and dance. Far from being an antisex prude, Miriam also sought to reconnect Moses and his Midianite/Cushite wife by taking on a larger share of leadership responsibilities.

Zelophehad's daughters marched directly up to the tent of meeting, unlike Cozbi and Zimri, who walked by it on their way to the *qubbah* shrine. Cozbi was a pawn in a patriarchal game to trick the Israelites into worshiping a foreign god. Balak and Balaam used her sexuality, and that of the other Moabite and Midianite women, in service to the patriarchy for their own purposes to further their own power and wealth. The Israelite women Mahlah, Tirzah, Hoglah, Milcah, and Noah brought their case against patriarchal rules that prevented them from having land allotted to them and their potential descendants. They took their case to Moses, the elders, the high priest, the whole community, and God. And the God of the Israelites pronounced that they were correct. In a manner of speaking, they drove a spear directly into the belly of androcentric inheritance laws. Equity is still a long time in coming, for sure, but certainly their bold appeal for gender justice led to increased economic opportunities for women.

> **Their bold appeal for gender justice led to increased economic opportunities for women.**

The women faced with the Sotah ritual were essentially the opposite of Cozbi. Instead of using her sexuality to serve a foreign god, the wife who participated in the Sotah was appealing to God to defend her sexuality against unsupported accusations by her husband. Cozbi took Zimri into a closed tent shrine, whereas the Sotah wife sought to have God witness that nothing untoward had happened in her tent or any other. Cozbi sought to deceive by means of sexuality, but the Sotah wife sought to establish the truth about her sexuality.

In these stories of women from and in the wilderness, Numbers presents several examples of righteous women: a prophet/ leader, gender justice advocates, and women who just wanted to be freed from suspicion and accusations about their sexuality. Yet no matter how explicit the biblical texts are in witnessing to women's leadership, their faithfulness, and their full humanity, patriarchal analogs of Zelophehad's uncles appear in every age and try to restrain, limit, disempower, and marginalize women.

In the same way, women in the body of Christ have had their initial privileges and responsibilities later constrained by men and patriarchal interpreters. Jesus had women disciples (Matt 27:55; Luke 8:1–3; Mark 15:40–41), and Paul worked with women church leaders and apostles (Chloe, 1 Cor 1:11; Nympha, Col 4:15; Apphia, Philem 2; Junia, Rom 16:7). But there remain those who would use a narrowly focused prohibition of ritual subjugation of men as part of a protognostic Ephesian Artemis cult in 1 Timothy 2:12 to prohibit women from teaching men anywhere, even in congregations in otherwise affirming denominations.[18] How much more horror do we need to uncover through the testimonies in the #MeToo and #ChurchToo movements before we recommit to leaving falsely comforting normalcy and head back into the wilderness to find out what God wants to tell us about how to love all our neighbors?

Numbers presents the stories of women who were not content with the status quo but sought to lead and change Israelite society for the better. The final chapter of this book seeks to address some of the ways that God's people have moved on and continue to move on from the revelation of God to holy action. The wilderness's unsettling of our lives allows opportunities to contemplate not just Scripture but our lives in new ways. With renewed vision, we are called to move forward.

GUIDED REFLECTIONS

1. What ideas or ways of living that you once considered settled or that you took for granted might God be calling you to reevaluate in a holy/weird way?

2. The stories of Miriam, Zelophehad's daughters, and even the Sotah ritual may seem removed from our everyday experience. But what can we learn from these wilderness stories? What stories of injustice have you seen or experienced?

3. How have you been or can you be an advocate for equality?

5

Place of Moving Forward

Then the Lord said to Moses, "Why do you cry out to me?
Tell the Israelites to go forward."

—Exodus 14:15

Except for small bands of prophets, wilderness experiences are not places where we dwell forever. The wilderness is a place where we go, or are forced to go, in order to encounter God outside of normal life. Most of the time, when we hear from God in our wilderness experiences, it is with a message to take back to our normal lives. God gives us a message about how to move forward. This message can take different forms and is not always a prophetic word. More frequently, we leave the wilderness having had a healing experience, a deeper intimacy with God, a new level of faith, changed perspectives, or even unmet expectations that challenge and agitate us. In any case, we do not leave the wilderness as the same person who entered. This was especially true for the Israelites. The community was not static and unchanging in

the wilderness; they moved and, I dare say, grew at the prerogative of the Lord. We, too, can use this wilderness moment in our
changing world or the wilderness moments in our individual
lives in order to focus on God's word and how we can move forward in light of God's love, justice, and mercy.

This last chapter focuses on some unexpected ways in which
God's people have moved forward in the midst of their wilderness
experiences and how they have shown us possible ways forward
as well.

I reference several examples of extrabiblical literature in this
chapter. Most of it was in existence around the time of Jesus, and
it was certainly known and cited by the early Christian community. If you can stay with me, I think that you may be surprised
by how closely it hews to the biblical text itself and how even the
inspired authors of Scripture relied on the extrabiblical material.

Waiting by the Red/Reed Sea

When we think of the Israelites arriving at the edge of the Red
Sea, we imagine Moses lifting his staff in his hands and the waters
immediately parting so that the Israelites can rush through and
the pursuing Egyptian army is drowned when the wall of water
crashes down upon them. The drama of this scene occludes some
crucial details in the biblical text.

For starters, in the Hebrew account, the name of the sea in
question is not the Red Sea but the Reed Sea. This is not, as some
have supposed, a copyist's error in the English. "Red Sea" is an
accurate translation of the Septuagint's *Erythra Thalassa* rather

than the Hebrew *Yam Suph*. But much more than the names of bodies of water is at stake in a close reading of the account at the Reed Sea. The reeds matter! One of my favorite passages of Scripture contrasts Moses's reverential waiting on the Lord with the behavior that God really wanted. As the Israelites waited for instructions at the Sea of Reeds, they looked up and saw the Egyptians approaching and cried out in fear. Then Moses responded:

> But Moses said to the people, "Do not be afraid, stand firm, and see the deliverance that the Lord will accomplish for you today; for the Egyptians whom you see today you shall never see again. The Lord will fight for you, and you have only to keep still."
>
> Then the Lord said to Moses, "Why do you cry out to me? Tell the Israelites to go forward." (Exod 14:13–15)

Many times in Scripture, wisdom teaches us to be still and wait on the Lord. This is not one of those cases. God wanted the people to move forward into the heart of the dangerous sea. The people were frightened of the Egyptians, but the pillar of smoke and fire acted as their rear guard and lit their way while they crossed the dry ground of the seabed all night (Exod 14:19–24).

Moses was God's friend (Exod 33:11), the humblest man of his generation (Num 12:3), and an excellent leader. But he was not perfect. Not all of his leadership was good (Exod 18:17–24), and it was his own disregard for God's holiness that prevented him and Aaron from entering the Holy Land (Num 20). In the case of the Israelites at the side of the Reed Sea, Moses gave bad advice. God wanted the Israelites to move forward.

I was reflecting on this while I watched news coverage of the 2017 white nationalist rally in Charlottesville. There is much benefit to praying and seeking the will of the Lord from where we are. I am most grateful for my clergy friends, including some of my former classmates and students, who did not abandon the public square to evil that day but went to Charlottesville to offer a peaceful counterwitness of the justice and universal love of God. They went forward into harm's way because they were convicted that they were called to be the visible body of Christ in public.

> They . . . were called to be the visible body of Christ in public.

God's people have always been putting their bodies and lives on the line, acting out courageous resistance against the evil powers, principalities, and rulers of this world (Eph 6:12) that have perpetuated racism, white supremacy, pride, and idolatry. Let us not forget that in Charlottesville, neo-Nazis and Klansmen assembled to protest the removal of a statue of General Robert E. Lee. We know from the Ten Commandments that any and all graven images are against God's will (Exod 20:4). I would argue that wherever graven images have been made to celebrate evil (slaveholding society), they are especially wrong. And when people resort to violence against other living humans to protect statues, they are especially wrong. However, wherever there has been a celebration of injustice or suffering, God's people have been there, witnessing against it. Countering racial injustice in the United States, Nazism and totalitarianism overseas, and colonialism and slavery wherever they have appeared, *some* of God's people have worked to resist and undermine this evil.[1]

However, too often the body of Christ has been slow to act against evil and even propped up evil systems, such as chattel slavery in the United States. In our own day, people who identify as Christian cry out Nazi slogans of "blood and soil," forgetting that their Messiah is Jewish and that he reached out across ethnic boundaries to show God's love to Samaritans, Canaanites, and Romans. God's community, even in the time of the wilderness wanderings, was not only composed of "pure" Israelites but also included a mixed multitude that was welcomed to join the going out from Egypt (Exod 12:38).

Some commentaries equate the mixed multitude of the Egyptians and other folks who had seen the power of God and wanted to join the Israelites in their quest to worship God with a grumbling crowd in Numbers 11:4. This position lacks scriptural support, however. The mixed multitude that exited Egypt with the Israelites was almost certainly not the same group that grumbled in Numbers 11:4 because different Hebrew terms are used for the two groups. We, as people who read God's word, need to be especially careful to not be led astray by poor expositions of the Bible that would seek to marginalize or exclude people whom God has already welcomed into community. Instead, we always need to submit biblical interpretations to what we know of God's loving character.

As an example, my wife attended a spiritually abusive church. She was confronted by toxic passivity as she tried to speak out about the lies that were being told and the people who were being hurt. When she raised the issues inside the church, she was told to "pray about it and let God change the hearts of the leaders." When she raised the issues of her church within the larger denomination, she was told to do nothing "because God cares more about the situation than any of us could."

In both cases, the leaders told her not to take action and refused to act to address the ongoing abuse. They attempted to shift the responsibility to God to intervene directly. Often this response reflects a lack of knowledge, confidence, or experience on the part of the leader about *how* to address the problem. So rather than learn or try, they abdicate responsibility for actively caring for the flock entrusted to them and encourage others to do the same.

Moses—God's chosen leader, God's friend, and God's prophet to the Israelites—fell short of what God desired in the instance by the Reed Sea. This does not mean that Moses was bad or evil, just that he was human. God called for him to act differently, and Moses immediately got to work. Moses was just slow to do what God wanted, making assumptions and relying on past experience rather than an ongoing discernment. There was one man, however, according to Jewish tradition, who was quick to spring into action to enact God's deliverance. His name was Nahshon.

Even from what we know from his brief appearances in the Bible, Nahshon was an important man—but one that most of us have never heard of. Nahshon was the prince of the tribe of Judah. Even though Judah was fourth in birth order, Nahshon was the first to present his offering for the temple on behalf of his tribe (Num 7:12). Aaron the priest married Nahshon's sister Elisheva, thus uniting through marriage the tribes of Levi and Judah (Exod 6:23). Later Jewish wisdom seizes on the mention of Elisheva as Nahshon's sister to advise that when considering a marriage partner, one should look to his or her siblings to understand the character of their potential children on the assumption that sons behave like their uncles (BT *Bava Batra* 110a). Aaron displayed wisdom in choosing a wife from a righteous family. Nahshon himself had several righteous descendants as well. He was an ancestor of David (1 Chr 2:11–15) and, accordingly, an ancestor of Jesus (Matt 1:4; Luke 3:32).

As important as Nahshon is in the Bible, his greatest importance in the history of God's people is only told in extrabiblical literature. Even if you are unsure about the veracity of Jewish holy writings outside the Hebrew Bible, these stories are worth our attention because they describe how people have conceived of God working through humans throughout sacred history.

As an example, as an anthropologist of religion, if I were to simply read the New Testament and then look for the roots of all the contemporary behaviors and beliefs of Protestant Christians in the United States, I would be bewildered. I would also need to consider the early ecumenical councils, the Great Schism, the Protestant Reformation, the Inquisitions, the Great Awakening, the Azusa Street revival and reactions to it, the Jesus People movement, and even Christian literature like the Left Behind series that have shaped, molded, encouraged, and disgusted people as they developed their understandings of what God is doing and what God has been up to for the last couple thousand years. This is where the rubber meets the road and the word of

Scripture is read, interpreted, applied, and ignored in the world. In the same way, Jewish extrabiblical literature, even if one does not regard it as sacred Scripture, demonstrates the faithful, loving, wise, and frequently cunning interpretations of sages who have a more intimate relationship with the text than all but a few Christians. As such, it is a profoundly useful and beautiful source of commentary for those who engage with it.

First, a careful reading of the biblical text shows that the splitting of the sea was not instantaneous. God told Moses to lift up his staff and stretch out his hand over the sea to divide it so that the Israelites could walk between the water on dry ground (Exod 14:16). But according to the text, Moses did not do it right away. First, the pillar of fire switched position from the front of the camp to be their rear guard. We are told that the two camps, Israelite and Egyptian, did not approach each other all night (Exod 14:20). It is only at this point, after the cloud of God's presence had moved and sometime during the long night, that the text says, "*Then* Moses stretched out his hand over the sea. The Lord drove the sea back by a strong east wind *all night*, and turned the sea into dry land; and the waters were divided" (Exod 14:21; emphasis added). The parting of the waters was not an instantaneous act, but God used an east wind to divide the waters over the course of the night. Moses's staff raising was not immediate. The separating of the waters was also not immediate. But Nahshon's obedience was immediate.

According to several rabbinic sources (Mechilta, Beshalach 6; Pirkei d'Rabbi Eliezer 42; Exodus Rabbah 13; and BT *Sotah* 37a, among others), Nahshon moved ahead in faith at the

Lord's command to move forward, not waiting for Moses to act. God said, "Tell the Israelites to move forward." And so that is exactly what Nahshon did, straight into the sea. Nahshon walked into the dark waters at night, alone. All Israel shifted their eyes from Moses to look at this one man who acted immediately to fulfill God's commandment that the Israelites should move forward. Nahshon, whose name means "ocean wave," entered the sea up to his knees, and nothing happened. He waded in up to his hips, and the cold water did not part. The water lapped at his chest, and still nothing happened. Deciding that fulfilling the word of the Lord was preferable to a life of fear waiting for others to obey God's commands, Nahshon sunk deeper into the water until the waves covered his mouth and nose, condemning him to drown. He had walked until his feet were tangled in the seaweed and reeds that give the sea its Hebrew name. It was only at that moment that the Holy One pushed the waters to the sides and made a path for Nahshon and the rest of the Israelites to cross to safety. For his faithfulness in being the sole Israelite to act out what God had called them to, he was given the opportunity to present the first offering to the Lord for the tabernacle and was included among the seventy elders who prophesied in Numbers 11. Further, the rabbis understood that King David was remembering his relative Nahshon when he used the sea imagery in Psalm 69:

> Save me, O God; for the waters are come in unto my soul.
> I sink in deep mire, where there is no standing: I am come
>   into deep waters, where the floods overflow me.

> Deliver me out of the mire, and let me not sink: let me be
> delivered from them that hate me, and out of the
> deep waters.
> Let not the waterflood overflow me, neither let the deep
> swallow me up, and let not the pit shut her mouth
> upon me. (Ps 69:1–2, 14–15 KJV)

King David meditated on the faith of Nahshon in order to discern how God might be calling David forward through his own wilderness experiences.

I believe that Nahshon should serve as an example for us in our world. We are not to charge blindly into every situation. That is not what Nahshon did, according to the rabbinic sources. He heard the Lord's command to the people to move forward. Because he was a prince, Nahshon could have commanded others to go forward first, but he boldly decided to lead from the front and entered the frightening waters, at night, by himself. He simply did what God had commanded and did not waver, even when he was at the point of drowning. I am sure it seemed like madness to Nahshon himself, and even more so to all those watching as he gradually disappeared beneath the waves.

Following God can be dangerous.

Following God can be dangerous. God's people have regularly been mocked, persecuted, and even killed for their faith. We need look no further than Jesus to see that doing God's will can be fatal. Thousands of martyrs have taken up their literal and figurative crosses and followed him over the ages. Following God is foolishness according to this world (1 Cor 1:18; 4:10). In the case of Nahshon, he survived his encounter with the sea. But he was prepared to die in his faithfulness to the Lord's commands. Even the threat of death itself can offer an opportunity to move forward in the wilderness times.

Deaths of the Leaders

Miriam the Prophet

It was inevitable that even the leaders of the wilderness generation died. Nahshon, Miriam, Aaron, and even Moses died in the wilderness before entering the promised land. We frequently skip over these details when thinking about the Israelites transitioning from wandering in the wilderness to entering the promised land. Most Christians, if they think about it at all, think that after forty years of wandering, the Israelites went straight to the battle of Jericho. But the book of Numbers records several important transitions, explaining how the camp moved forward in spite of, or even because of, loss. I want to take a look at the deaths of Miriam and Moses in order to explore how God's intimacy during times of loss and letting go can help us move forward and advance God's kingdom.

Miriam's role as a prophet (Exod 15:20) was but one of the reasons that her death in the wilderness was mourned by all of Israel. We also read that immediately after Miriam's death, the Israelites faced a major problem: "Then the sons of Israel, the whole congregation, came to the wilderness of Zin in the first month; and the people stayed at Kadesh. Now Miriam died there and was buried there. There was no water for the congregation, and they assembled against Moses and Aaron" (Num 20:1–2 NASB). It seems strange to move right from Miriam's death to there being no water for the Israelites. Were these things connected? How had the Israelites been getting their drinking water?

Way back in Exodus 17:6, when the Israelites complained of thirst, God told Moses to strike a rock, and it gushed forth water. The wilderness journey would not include another request for water until after Miriam died. Sometimes the Israelite camp was in places like Elim (Exod 15:27), where there were twelve springs. But many other times, they were in the actual desert without water. The Israelites certainly did not hold back their complaints when they had to go without something, so it seems like they probably had enough water to drink on an ongoing basis.

Jewish legend says that the source of water accompanied the Israelites on their journey. It is understood, and depicted in artwork, as a rock with holes in it that rolled after the camp (Tosefta Sukkah 3:11; see Exod 17:6 and Num 20). Paul the apostle knew of this tradition of the traveling rock as a water supply and saw it as an allusion to Jesus providing living water (1 Cor 10:4).

The sages posited that the traveling rock dried up when Miriam died because it was only after she died that the Israelites cried out again in thirst. Something about Miriam's death led to the end of their water supply. The sages further inferred that it was not just Miriam's death that closed the well but her praises that opened it. Just as her death was recounted immediately before the people cried out in thirst in Numbers 20, so her praises were recounted before an earlier provision of the water in Exodus 15:

> Then the prophet Miriam, Aaron's sister, took a tambourine in her hand; and all the women went out after her with tambourines and with dancing. And Miriam sang to them:
>
>> "Sing to the Lord, for he has triumphed gloriously; horse and rider he has thrown into the sea."
>
> Then Moses ordered Israel to set out from the Red Sea, and they went into the wilderness of Shur. They went three days in the wilderness and found no water. When they came to Marah, they could not drink the water of Marah because it was bitter. That is why it was called Marah [bitter]. And the people complained against Moses, saying, "What shall we drink?" He cried out to the Lord; and the Lord showed him a piece of wood; he threw it into the water, and the water became sweet. (Exod 15:20–25)

The ancient biblical commenters reasoned that if Miriam's death closed off the water from the rock, maybe Miriam had also done something just prior to the opening of the rock. Her leadership of the community in grateful praise to the Lord was still ringing in God's ears when the people cried out for water. For this reason, the miraculous provision of water during most of the wilderness journey is simply known as Miriam's Well (BT *Ta'anit* 9a).

When Miriam died, the water ran out. A great leader, one beloved of the people and of God, had died and was no longer around to shepherd the people. The Israelite camp, however, had no other choice but to continue their journey. They did have a choice, however, in what manner they moved forward. Would they be like Miriam and pursue the Lord with grateful praise? The sad answer is no, they would not, at least not yet. The people not only were ungrateful for God's previous provision of water, but they assembled themselves against Moses and Aaron and contended against them (Num 20:2). This Israelite rebellion against Moses and Aaron finally provoked Moses to the rash action that would lead to the deaths of Miriam's brothers outside the promised land.

> **Would they be like Miriam and pursue the Lord with grateful praise?**

Moses the Friend of God

At the end of the Israelites' wilderness journey, their great leader, champion, and prophet Moses died, along with their first high priest, Aaron. Moses had been the one to announce God's will that they should worship God at the holy mountain and then enter the Holy Land. But Moses was to die in sight of, but outside, the land to which he had brought his people. This death sounds tragic to us. Moses led the people to freedom, but he would die without the ultimate reward for his years of faithfulness. But that is not what the Bible really says. The account of Moses's death and the events surrounding it occur in a few places in Scripture. I want to start with the most complete version. In Deuteronomy, we are told that Moses surveyed the land and then died:

> Then Moses went up from the plains of Moab to Mount Nebo, to the top of Pisgah, which is opposite Jericho, and the Lord showed him the whole land. . . . Then the Lord said to him, "This is the land which I swore to Abraham, Isaac, and Jacob, saying, 'I will give it to your descendants'; I have let you see with your eyes, but you shall not go over there." So Moses the servant of the Lord died there in the land of Moab, *according to the mouth of the Lord*. And He buried him in the valley in the land of Moab, opposite Beth-peor; but no man knows his burial place to this day. Although Moses was one hundred and twenty years old when he died, his eye was not dim, nor his vigor abated. So the sons of Israel wept for Moses in the plains of Moab thirty days; then the days of tearful mourning for Moses came to an end. (Deut 34:1, 4–8)

At first glance, this seems like a straightforward passage. Moses was allowed to see the promised land, and then he died. But there is a very interesting detail in how he died: he died at the mouth of God. Many Bibles will translate *peh* as "word" or "command," but most have a footnote pointing out the actual Hebrew meaning of the passage. It is from this passage that the rabbis understood that Moses, along with his siblings, died from a kiss from the Lord (Deuteronomy Rabbah 11:10; Num 33:38).

There is an elegant symmetry between the death of Moses that ends the Torah and the creation story that began God's relationship with humans way back in Genesis 1 and 2. God breathed souls into the faces of humans at the beginning (Gen 2:7), and God received the soul of Moses through a kiss at the end of his life. Moreover, just as God took the human from the clay at the beginning, so did God personally return Moses to the earth in burial (Deut 34:6). God personally saw to the burial of God's friend, Moses.

> The point of the story of Moses's death is that God loved Moses as a friend.

But a divine burial and death by a gentle kiss were not the only special honors accorded to Moses at his death, according to the Jewish sources. Even as his death approached, evil spiritual forces sought to hasten his end or desecrate his body, but God sent God's angels, including Michael and Gabriel, to defend Moses's soul and body. This story is preserved in many places, including Midrash *Petirat Moshe* and also the New Testament book of Jude, where we read, "But Michael the archangel, when he disputed with the devil and argued about the body of Moses, did not dare pronounce against him a railing judgment, but said, 'The Lord rebuke you!'" (Jude 9 NASB). The stories of Miriam's and Moses's deaths were all familiar to first-century Jews, and indeed, Jude even incorporated part of Moses's extrabiblical story into what eventually became a letter of the New Testament. And for good reason, these stories have much to teach us if we are willing to learn from them.

The point of the story of Moses's death is that God loved Moses as a friend. Even when Moses was punished for his disobedience with a death outside of the Holy Land, it was a death lovingly presided over by Moses's friend, God. The gentle death of Moses provided an opportunity for the Israelites to move forward out of the wilderness and into the next phase of their journey: "Now Joshua the son of Nun was filled with the spirit of wisdom, for Moses had laid his hands on him; and the sons of Israel obeyed him and did as the Lord had commanded Moses" (Deut 34:9 NASB).

The Israelites offer an example to us in responding to difficult times in our lives, especially wilderness moments that produce sadness, confusion, and disorientation. Of course it is right to mourn when bad things happen. But even punishment from God frequently comes as loving discipline, as a parent disciplines a beloved daughter or son (Heb 12:6–7). Even death is not the end of God's love but eventually will be put to an end in Christ (1 Cor 15:55). As God leads us through wilderness journeys, sometimes we may be asked to let go of something, or even someone, that we are tempted to hold on to. Obviously, this is not always the death of a beloved guide. In my own life, one of the biggest struggles in a particular wilderness time was letting go of a harmful and ultimately untrue self-image that had been pounded into my brain and heart by childhood bullies and false friends. But even when we lose someone we love and are thrust into a wilderness place of not being able to imagine what life could possibly be without them, we remember who God is. In death, God welcomes with a kiss when the time comes, and we trust and look forward to God awakening us and our loved ones again at the resurrection. Until the end of our earthly lives, we do well to push forward, like the Israelites.

Death of the Righteous

The death of Miriam, the death of Aaron, and the description of the action that leads to Moses's death all occur in a section of the Torah that is called *Chukat*, or "decrees." It opens with the description of the ordeal of the red heifer in Numbers 19, which provides atonement for the uncleanliness that comes from exposure to death. In fact, the death of Miriam immediately follows the description of how to purify from death.

The rabbis posited that the description of the death of an exceptional being (the red heifer) that was able to atone for sin and purify Israel flowed naturally into the story of the deaths of Miriam, Aaron, and Moses. The connection between these passages was not coincidental. The rabbis understood that the death of righteous Miriam, Aaron, and Moses atoned for the sins of many (BT *Mo'ed Katan* 28a). The concept of the death of the righteous atoning for many will not be unfamiliar to Christian readers.

> A righteous person's prayerful intercession . . . can be very effective indeed.

The idea that a person's righteousness can move God on behalf of others is visible in both testaments of the Bible, yet many Christians seem resistant to this idea. The book that bears the name of one of Jesus's siblings and the reputed head of the Jerusalem church instructed believers, "Pray for one another so that you may be healed. The effective prayer of a righteous man can accomplish much" (Jas 5:16 NASB). A righteous person's prayerful intercession on behalf of another can be very effective indeed.

In the Hebrew Bible, when the Israelites had committed the sins around the golden calf, God told Moses that God was abandoning the people. Moses, however, intervened and requested that if he had found favor in God's sight, God should lead the people into the promised land (Exod 33:12–13). God sought to negotiate and said, "My presence shall go . . . and I will give you [singular] rest" (Exod 33:14). God only indicated God's presence moving and that only Moses would receive rest. Moses saw God's offer for what it was and insisted in the next verse, "If your presence does not go . . . do not lead *us* up from here" (Exod 33:15 NASB; emphasis added). God's response after a little more pressure from Moses in verse 16 was to finally agree in gracious terms to go with the whole people, specifically because God's friend Moses insisted: "The Lord said to Moses, 'I will also do this thing of which you have spoken; for you have found favor in My sight and I have known you by name'" (Exod 33:17 NASB). Thus after the terrible sin of the golden calf, Moses was able to rely on the friendship he had with God and the favor with which God viewed him to intercede on behalf of the people. Intercession of the righteous is a well-established pattern, and we should not be surprised that Miriam's and Aaron's deaths are linked to methods of atonement for the whole people. We Christians look to another to save us from our sins for all time.

In Hebrews 13, Jesus himself is compared to the red heifer, which, unlike other sacrifices, was burnt outside of the camp (vv. 11–13). The notion that the death of the righteous somehow saves others is central to our faith. Jesus, more than even the children of Amram and Jochebed, led God's people from slavery to freedom. In our everyday lives, Jesus is taking us on a journey through the wilderness, from a place of bondage to sin and death to a holy city (Heb 11:10). Like Miriam and Moses, Jesus experienced great intimacy with God after his death (though certainly more than they could imagine, being the Incarnate Son). More than these others, after Jesus's resurrection, he was welcomed to the right hand of God (Luke 22:69). His death and resurrection show us the way forward from rejecting our slavery to sin to moving through a wilderness where we seek to hear from God. Ultimately, we will settle in eternal homes (John 14:2), but for now, we still journey forward in this world. The last section reflects on some of the saints before us who have forged a path through their own wildernesses.

Desert Mothers and Fathers

One of the prime ways that we make our way forward in this soteriological wilderness after Jesus saved us but before God renews all things is by figuring out how to be Christlike in our behavior toward our brothers and sisters. I want to think about, for the last time in this book, how we do that in our communities. Over one thousand years after the Israelite experience in the wilderness, a group of early Christians sought out wilderness experiences to figure out how to live the reality of Christ's presence in their lives without bowing to the demands of empire. We know them as the desert mothers and fathers.

While he was far from the first Christian to seek out life in the wilderness, Saint Anthony (also known as Anthony the Great) popularized a life of poverty in an unforgiving wilderness as a means of approaching God. His biographer, Athanasius of Alexandria, recounted that he heard a sermon on Sunday on the rich, young ruler. Jesus's response struck a chord in him: "If you wish to be perfect, go, sell your possessions, and give the money to the poor, and you will have treasure in heaven; then come, follow me" (Matt 19:21). Saint Anthony sold all that he had, gave a small amount of the profits to his sister, and gave the rest to the poor. He then headed out to the wilderness places to learn about how to follow Jesus in a path of self-sacrifice.

By most accounts, Anthony headed into the desert in 271 CE. While he journeyed to different places, his life was spent mostly outside the places of regular settlement. He was by no means alone, however. Thousands came out to learn from this man who had turned his back on living within the places controlled by empire. Thousands came to the desert to live simply together in small communes or independently. The people who came to learn and worship with him brought news of the outside world. They told Anthony of the great persecution begun by Diocletian in 303 and also of Constantine I's promulgation of the Edict of Milan (313), legalizing the practice of Christianity in the Roman Empire.

Anthony chose to continue his ascetic life and pursuit of faith rather than participate in the new government-granted freedom of the empire. Unlike many Christian martyrs whose deaths testified to their love of God and God's holiness, the desert Christians chose to pray, fast, and study Scripture in peace and relative safety.

They embraced the life that they felt moved forward the worship and knowledge of God through Jesus. The deaths of the saints were indeed precious to God (Ps 116:15), but so are their lives. It is my firm belief that, to paraphrase the words of Paul, if they lived, they lived for the Lord, and if they died, they died for the Lord (Rom 14:8).

As persecution of Christianity ebbed and flowed, many early Christians chose to maintain their everyday lives and community connections, knowing that they risked persecution and possible death to spread the message of the risen Messiah. Many others chose to flee persecution to live in faithful communities in the wilderness. Both choices honored God during a period of hostility.

Thankfully, these early persecutions ended. The emperor embraced the name of Jesus, if not his pacific ways, and the practice of Christianity was made legal. The desert Christians did not return from their dwellings in the wilderness, however. Knowing that ease can be deadlier to love and devotion to God than persecution, they rejected the embrace of empire and remained outside society. Indeed, the popularity of desert Christianity expanded after 313 and the Edict of Milan. Ease, prosperity, and lack of hardship have always been threats to faithfulness to God. It is for this reason that the Israelites were warned by God through Moses that they should remember how God led them through the wilderness when they were settled in the land and had homes and plenty of fruit, grain, and water (Deut 8:16–18). It is too easy to think we are self-sufficient when all we need for life is easily accessible (Deut 8:11–14).

Anthony took this warning seriously and embraced words quoted by Jesus, that one does not live by bread alone but by every word that comes from the mouth of God (Deut 8:3; Matt 4:4). But Anthony and the desert mothers and fathers did not just sell their possessions and sit idly. They were active in praying, singing psalms, studying Scriptures, and teaching in community, and they engaged in manual labor that allowed their small communities to provide for their few needs.

The size of the community depended on the philosophy of the people involved. Anthony and others like him preferred to live as hermits. Again, this is not to say that he never interacted with other humans. Rather, his fundamental experience of life was one alone with God, but he is renowned for his hospitality and warm reception of visitors and pilgrims. The semihermits, such as Saint Amun, spent most of their days in solitude but regularly met with brothers and sisters to worship and exchange wisdom. The cenobites, such as Pachomius, formed small communities in which members ate, studied, and worked communally, but away from larger society.

Above all, these different types of communities scrupulously avoided making an idol of the solitary life. One of the desert fathers was recorded telling his friend that he intended to live in his tiny cell alone and would never interact with another human until his death. His friend responded that unless he was able to amend his life for the better around his brothers and sisters, he would never be able to amend his life alone.[2] The flip side of this rejection of practical solipsism, however, was a deep concentration on the mind of God, to the exclusion of what society deemed as important. Another saying of the community may clarify this.

A young man came out to a desert father, Abba Macarius, and asked if he could become holy in one day. The father thought for a moment and then agreed to try. He told the young man that he should go into the local cemetery and insult the dead with every wickedness that he could think of—yell obscenities, hit their graves with a stick, and dishonor their memories. The young man went and did so and returned to the father at the end of the day. The father asked, When you abused the holy dead, what did they say to you? The young man replied that they had said nothing because they were dead. The father then said that he would require one more day to make the young man holy,

> **Focus on the word of the Lord, which calls you "son" or "daughter."**

and he agreed. The next morning, the father urged the young man to go to the cemetery and heap every sort of praise on the deceased—honoring them, their works, their families, and their graves. The young man did so and returned to the father at the end of the second day. The father asked him, What did the holy departed say to you when you blessed and honored them? Confused, the young man responded that they did not say anything because they were dead. The father replied that this was the path to holiness: ignore equally those who curse and praise you, for this is without meaning. Instead, focus on the word of the Lord, which calls you "son" or "daughter." Escape from dependence on the views of humans and focus on the thoughts of God. Do this to be holy.[3]

The desert mothers and fathers sought to love other humans from a place of nondependency on earthly things. They reasoned that only when one sought nothing from another could they really love selflessly, as Christ loved the church. This cuts to the core of my heart. I seek to serve my wife and sons daily, making them breakfast and dinner and rubbing my wife's feet at the end of each day after she chases our children around the house. I feel good about loving my family in these ways. But I want something back. I want my wife's praise. I want her to tell me (and all her Facebook friends) what a good husband she has. I want honor and praise. I do not take the early shift with our children and cook her breakfast when she wakes up solely because I want to receive thanks. But I would be lying if I said that I do not care whether I am thanked or not. I am trying to get over this, to be as the young man and care not for the praise or critiques of men (and my special woman). But it is so difficult! In order to avoid the constant flow of praise and shame, the desert Christians went out to the wilderness. Outside of the patterns of normal life, they were less subject to persecution but also less subject to acclaim. They chose to move away from normal life and embrace simply praising and honoring God from humble poverty.

There is wisdom here for me, and maybe for you as well. I am on a closed Facebook clergy group in which many of us share sermon ideas with each other. It is difficult to come up with a speech every week in addition to caring for the flock and doing all the nonpastoral work of running church councils/boards, maintaining buildings, and paying church bills as clergy often do. So we help each other. I am not a pastor yet, so I have different time constraints than most people in the group, but once in a while, I post what I think is an *amazing* interpretation and lesson from Scripture. A couple years ago, I posted some commentary that I was sure would be a super-helpful and popular interpretation of one of the lectionary passages for the upcoming week. I thought it would help the pastors in the Facebook group prepare sermons on a difficult passage of Scripture. After an overnight train trip to another country, during which my mobile phone died, I did not have access to the internet for about eighteen hours. Imagine my shock and horror two days later when I turned on my computer after forty-eight hours to find that there was only one measly "like" on my post in a group with thousands of daily participants. My ego was crushed! This would not have been the case if I were a successful desert father looking to God alone for my identity. But I am not. I am a temporary wilderness dweller doing my best to learn their ways.

In the meantime, I believe, aside from receiving honor and discipline solely from God, there is another lesson for us: refusing to participate in empire. This I am better at. I still fall prey to the whims of fickle and fleeting social media popularity and obscurity, but I resist, as much as possible, letting political or national affiliation define me. On that same train ride years ago, a temporary friend asked if I was scared to live in Morocco after Moroccans had committed several acts of terror in Barcelona a few days earlier (the 2017 Barcelona attacks). I said I was not especially afraid. I asked my Moroccan fellow passenger on the train if he was scared. He said yes, a little, because you just never know when someone is going to do something crazy. I agreed. We never know what our neighbors are contemplating. Whether it is Barcelona, Nice, Jerusalem, or Charlottesville, acts of political violence are possible everywhere.

I will not let terrorists or presidents control my thoughts and feelings and make me suspicious of a race, nationality, or religion.

My head and my heart belong to God. Similarly, I will not let political parties decide how I should feel about issues and, more importantly, how I interact with other human beings. Please do not misunderstand me: There are those who fight for justice within the political realm, and I think this work is a holy act. There are those who fight for justice outside the political realm, and I think that is a holy act as well.

My fight, however, is to love the people whom I see day-to-day on the street wherever I live, and my choice is to identify and enter the struggles of the people in my neighborhood. Part of that is trying to support my family. Most of it is simply looking in the faces of people experiencing homelessness and greeting them with as much respect and love as I greet the policewoman who lives near me. I engage in the daily struggle to shun what empire would demand, to protect what is ours and add to it. Instead, I try (and mostly fail, but still try) to give away the love of Jesus, and my resources along with it, to my neighbors in this wilderness place. Meister Eckhart, the medieval German theologian, said that the spiritual life is less about addition than subtraction.[4] Pastor Emmy Kegler wrote about how God took the Israelites out of slavery in a day but spent much longer taking the influences of slavery out of the Israelites.[5] I think they are right. When we subtract the influences of empire, social honor, and shame from our lives, we are freer to focus on how God would have us move forward in love and community.

> My choice is to identify and enter the struggles of the people in my neighborhood.

That is the work of Numbers and the time in the wilderness: to help us move to a point where we can break free of how the daily distractions in our normal lives hinder us from growing closer to God and each other.

One of my great hopes for you, dear reader, is that you would be inspired by the example of Nahshon. He was a prince and relatively comfortable in Egypt, presumably. He probably worked like all the other Israelites, but he was a respected and respectable man. He chose to lead his tribe into the wilderness with Moses because he saw the acts of God and yearned for freedom to worship. When the Israelites were pinned in between the Egyptian army and the sea, he did not complain or wish to go back to Egypt like many other Israelites. Instead, he simply went forward because that is what he heard God say to do. I bless you to seek out the word of God in Scripture, prayer, and communion with the saints, living and dead. And when you hear what God is calling you to, whatever that would be, I hope you will go forward and do it. In this, we have not just Nahshon to show us the way but Jesus, who "for the sake of the joy that was *set before him* endured the cross, disregarding its shame, and has taken his seat at the right hand of the throne of God" (Heb 12:2). May you endure and approach God's throne!

Miriam, Aaron, and Moses died while the Israelites were still in the wilderness. In Judaism, their lives and deaths served to save their community. For Christians, they serve as a sort of Jewish prefiguration of the Christian idea of the salvific work of Jesus. Their gentle deaths in the wilderness allowed the Israelite community occasions to reflect on their losses and move forward out of the wilderness and into a new reality in the way they honored their beloved deceased.

The desert mothers and fathers journeyed to the wilderness as a matter of choice and because they were driven there by persecution. In both cases, they used the opportunity to leave behind the trappings (read traps) of civilization, the opinions that bind, and the empire that crushes and flatters. They sought to live simple lives, studying God's word, providing for the poor, and pursuing intimacy with God through prayer and fasting. They chose a unique path forward. They neither suffered the persecutions of empire nor tried to thread that difficult needle of maintaining faithfulness to God while living under the reign of an earthly king. Their lives can help us consider the cost of comfort and the importance of taking Jesus's words seriously: "One does not live by bread alone, but by every word that comes from the mouth of God" (Matt 4:4), and "If you wish to be perfect, go, sell your possessions, and give the money to the poor, and you will have treasure in heaven; then come, follow me" (Matt 19:21).

The book of Numbers/*Bmidbar* is the perfect guide for us when we feel lost and confused. It does not contain the heady events of the exodus from Egyptian slavery, nor does it tell of the actual settling of the promised land. Instead, it is a book about the in-between time and how God and God's people get to know each other as they wander together in the wilderness place. That framing is important, as we frequently need to return to wilderness experiences. It may be that the only thing that comes of your wilderness journey is increased intimacy with God. The realities you left behind for a bit may be exactly the same when you return. Or things may have changed precipitously. Whatever the case, God is eager to bring you into a holy/weird/uncomfortable place and there to give you a vision of who God is and who you are and to enable you to move forward for God's kingdom. I hope this book has been helpful for you in your journey.

GUIDED REFLECTIONS

1. Nahshon and Moses offer two models for responding to God. In the context discussed in this chapter, Nahshon's way was preferred. However, many times in Scripture we are told to wait on God and obey God. How do you know which to do? What are some situations in your personal life where you ought to move forward? Where do you need to be still and cry out to the Lord?

2. What about your communal life? Where might you need to move or stand fast as one manifestation of the body of Christ?

3. Think of your favorite martyr, or even one of your own beloved deceased. How has her or his life and death shaped you? What strength does her or his faithfulness unto death give you?

4. Jesus, who scrupulously avoided being roped into insurrection against the Roman occupation, nonetheless testified to the weakness and passing frailty of empire by his surrender to and then victory over the powers of sin and death. How does being a follower of Jesus inspire you to resist the power, claim, and attraction of empire? What are the particular traps set by the empire in which you live?

5. Martin Luther offered a good and useful corrective to medieval monasticism, which had gotten away from simple lives devoted to prayer and care for the poor and instead focused on the accumulation of wealth and concentration of spiritual power and prestige. He argued that normal people's vocations were avenues to worship and honor God. Thinking back to the teaching of Abba Macarius about refusing to be swayed by either honor or shame and Jesus's own warning about positions and titles of honor (Matt 23:6–12), how can you in your job, your relations by choice (friends, loves), and your relations by blood actively shun honor, shame, and empire to love without dependency on others to define your self-image? Please send your best ideas to me!

NOTES

INTRODUCTION

1 "New MLA Survey Shows Significant Increases in Foreign Language Study at U.S. Colleges and Universities," Modern Language Association, November 13, 2007, https://www.mla.org/content/download/3048/80546/release11207_ma_feb_update.pdf.

2 *Middle East* is a problematic term because it assumes a Eurocentric perspective. One might ask, east of whom? In the middle of what? Therefore, just as we talk about other regions as continentally based locations (e.g., southern Africa, northern Europe, East Asia), I will use the term *Southwest Asia*.

3 See Brevard Childs, *Introduction to the Old Testament as Scripture* (Philadelphia: Fortress, 1979), 82–83; Brevard Childs, *Biblical Theology of the Old and New Testaments: Theological Reflection on the Christian Bible* (Minneapolis: Fortress, 1993), 672; and Phyllis Trible, *God and the Rhetoric of Sexuality* (Philadelphia: Fortress, 1978), 8.

4 See, for example, Rachel Held Evans, *Inspired: Slaying Giants, Walking on Water and Loving the Bible Again* (Nashville: Thomas Nelson, 2018).

CHAPTER 1

1 Avivah Gottlieb Zornberg, *Bewilderments: Reflections on the Book of Numbers* (New York: Schocken, 2015), 1.

2 The tent of meeting, previously outside of the community (Exod 33:7), was apparently to be brought into the midst of the people.

3 God says some variant of "I will be their God and they will be my people" at least forty-three times in Scripture.

4 Amy-Jill Levine and Ben Witherington III, *The Gospel of Luke* (Cambridge: Cambridge University Press, 2018), 487.

5 Genesis Rabbah 92:7.

6 More on why his understanding may have been incorrect in the following paragraphs.

7 Jon Levenson, *Death and Resurrection of the Beloved Son: The Transformation of Child Sacrifice in Judaism and Christianity* (Binghamton, NY: Yale University Press, 1993), 180–93.

8 Abraham Joshua Heschel, *The Prophets* (New York: Harper Perennial, 2001). For "theomorphism," see especially 349, and for "anthropotropism," see especially 562–67.

9 Jack Gilbert, *Refusing Heaven* (New York: Alfred A. Knopf, 2005), 3.

CHAPTER 2

1 Compare Hosea 2:14.

2 Katherine Doob Sakenfeld, "Numbers," in *Women's Bible Commentary*, ed. Carol Newsom, Sharon Ringe, and Jacqueline Lapsley (Louisville: Westminster John Knox, 2012), 85.

3 Dennis Olson, *Numbers* (Louisville: John Knox, 1996), 155.

4 Francis Brown, S. R. Driver, Charles A. Briggs, James Strong, and Wilhelm Gesenius, *The Brown-Driver-Briggs Hebrew and English Lexicon* (Peabody, MA: Hendrickson, 1996), 469.

5 Rodney Hutton, "Cozbi," in *The Anchor Bible Dictionary*, ed. D. N. Freedman (New York: Doubleday, 1992), 1202.

6 Anthony Rees, "[Re]naming Cozbi: In Memoriam, Cozbi, Daughter of Zur," *Biblical Interpretation: A Journal of Contemporary Approaches* 20, no. 1 (2012): 20–23.

7 Several rabbis saw the sexual euphemism "to bring close" (Gen 20:4 and Deut 22:14) and "for his brothers" as Zimri aiding the Midianite effort to induce Israel to mass orgy and afterward to mass idolatry. See Stephen Reif, "What Enraged Phinehas? A Study of Numbers 25:8," *Journal of Biblical Literature*, 90, no. 2 (1971): 203. Alternative readings suggest that Cozbi was being brought to Zimri's family tent for marriage. This seems unlikely, given the context of the chapter and especially the following verses.

8 Reif, 204–5.

9 Sakenfeld, in *Women's Bible Commentary*, for instance, titles the commentary on this section as "The Danger of Foreign Women" (85).

10 Helena Zlotnick, "A Woman of the Wilderness: The Rape of Cozbi," in *Dinah's Daughters: Gender and Judaism from the Hebrew Bible to Late Antiquity* (Philadelphia: University of Pennsylvania Press, 2002), 52; Susan Thistlethwaite, "'You May Enjoy the Spoil of Your Enemies': Rape as a Biblical Metaphor for War," *Semeia* 61 (1993): 62.

11 Numbers Rabbah 21:15, 13:20.

12 Graham Ward, "Bodies: The Displaced Body of Jesus Christ," in *Radical Orthodoxy: A New Theology*, ed. John Milbank, Catherine Pickstock, and Graham Ward (London: Routledge, 1999), 163–81.

13 Martin Luther, "The Estate of Marriage," in *Luther's Works: Christian in Society II*, vol. 45, ed. Walther I. Brandt (Philadelphia: Fortress, 1962), 39–40.

14 Dr. West's perhaps most frequently cited quote is ubiquitous at his guest lectures, such as at Harvard University's Graduate School of Education Askwith Forum on October 4, 2017.

15 "Report of the Sentencing Project to the United Nations Human Rights Committee regarding Racial Disparities in the United States Criminal Justice System," Sentencing Project, August 2013, http://sentencingproject.org/wp-content/uploads/2015/12/Race-and-Justice-Shadow-Report-ICCPR.pdf.

16 Arpit Gupta, Christopher Hansman, and Ethan Frenchman, "The Heavy Costs of High Bail: Evidence from Judge Randomization,"

Journal of Legal Studies 45, no. 2 (June 2016), http://www.journals.uchicago.edu/doi/full/10.1086/688907.

17 Gupta, Hansman, and Frenchman.

CHAPTER 3

1 Avivah Zornberg, "The Genesis of Desire," On Being with Krista Tippett, October 6, 2011, https://onbeing.org/programs/avivah-zornberg-the-genesis-of-desire/.

2 Zornberg, *Bewilderments*, 236. Zornberg notes that Rashi understood Balaam as "avaricious and covetous of [all] other peoples' wealth."

3 Margaret McKenna, "Mark 1: Relocation to Abandoned Places of Empire," in *School(s) for Conversion: 12 Marks of a New Monasticism*, ed. the Rutba House (Eugene, OR: Cascade, 2005), 22–24.

CHAPTER 4

1 Katharine Doob Sakenfeld, "Feminist Biblical Interpretation," *Theology Today* 46, no. 2 (July 1, 1989): 154.

2 Sakenfeld, 155.

3 Zornberg, *Bewilderments*, 93.

4 The rabbis insist that the Cushite woman is Zipporah and that she is called Cushite because her skin was exceptionally beautiful, like that of people from Cush/Ethiopia (*Tanhuma, Zav* 13).

5 For a meditation on how Miriam was a source of refreshment for her community, please see chapter 5.

6 Sakenfeld, "Feminist Biblical Interpretation," 156.

7 Sakenfeld, 167.

8 Phyllis Trible, "Biblical Views: Wrestling with Faith," *Biblical Archeology Review* 40, no. 5 (2014): 22.

9 Olson, *Numbers*, 36.

10 See Phyllis Trible, *Texts of Terror: Literary-Feminist Readings of Biblical Narratives* (Philadelphia: Fortress, 1983).

11 Brian Britt, "Male Jealousy and the Suspected Sotah: Toward a Counter-reading of Numbers 5:11–31," *The Bible and Critical Theory* 3, no. 1 (2011): 05.1.

12 Alice Bach, "Good to the Last Drop: Viewing the Sotah (Numbers 5:11–31) as the Glass Half Empty and Wondering How to View It Half Full," in *Women in the Hebrew Bible*, ed. Alice Bach (New York: Routledge, 1999), 506–7.

13 Bach, 505.

14 Jack Sasson, "Numbers 5 and the 'Waters of Judgement,'" in *Women in the Hebrew Bible*, ed. Alice Bach (New York: Routledge, 1999), 483.

15 Sasson, 483.

16 Sasson, 484.

17 Jacob Milgrom, *The JPS Torah Commentary: Numbers* (Philadelphia: Jewish Publication Society, 1990), 350.

18 Linda L. Belleville, "Teaching and Usurping Authority: 1 Timothy 2:11–15," in *Discovering Biblical Equality: Complementarity without Hierarchy*, ed. Ronald Pierce and Rebecca Merrill Groothuis (Downers Grove, IL: InterVarsity, 2004), 205–23; Mark Braun, "An Exegesis of 1 Timothy 2:11–15 and Its Relation to the CHE Statement: The Role of Man and Woman According to Holy Scripture," speech delivered to the Michigan District Southwestern Conference Pastoral Conference at Peace Lutheran Church, Otsego, MI, February 24, 1981; Catherine C. Kroeger, "Ancient Heresies and a Strange Greek Verb," *Reformed Journal* 29 (1979): 12–15; Catherine C. Kroeger and Richard C. Kroeger, *I Suffer Not a Woman: Rethinking 1 Timothy 2:11–15 in Light of Ancient Evidence* (Grand Rapids, MI: Baker Academic, 1981); Guy Maclean Rogers, *Mysteries of Artemis of Ephesos: Cult, Polis, and Change in the Graeco-Roman World* (New Haven, CT: Yale University Press, 2012), 425; Cynthia Long Westfall, *Paul and Gender: Reclaiming the Apostle's Vision for Men and Women in Christ* (Grand Rapids, MI: Baker Academic, 2016).

CHAPTER 5

1 Karen Fields, "Christian Missionaries as Anticolonial Militants," *Theory and Society* 11, no. 1 (1982): 98–105.

2 John Wortley, trans., *The Book of the Elders: Sayings of the Desert Fathers; The Systematic Collection* (Collegeville, MN: Liturgical Press, 2012), 99–100.

3 Benedicta Ward, trans., *The Sayings of the Desert Fathers: The Alphabetical Collection* (Kalamazoo, MI: Cistercian, 1975), 132.

4 Richard Rohr, "An Introduction to Francis of Assisi: A Spirituality of Subtraction," Center for Action and Contemplation, May 18, 2015, https://cac.org/a-spirituality-of-subtraction-2015-05-18/.

5 Emmy Kegler, *One Coin Found: How God's Love Stretches to the Margins* (Minneapolis: Fortress, 2019), 163.

SELECT BIBLIOGRAPHY

Bach, Alice. "Good to the Last Drop: Viewing the Sotah (Numbers 5:11–31) as the Glass Half Empty and Wondering How to View It Half Full." In *Women in the Hebrew Bible*, edited by Alice Bach, 503–522. New York: Routledge, 1999.

Britt, Brian. "Male Jealousy and the Suspected Sotah: Toward a Counter-reading of Numbers 5:11–31." *The Bible and Critical Theory* 3, no. 1 (2011): 05.1–05.19.

Childs, Brevard. *Introduction to the Old Testament as Scripture.* Philadelphia: Fortress, 1979.

Claiborne, Shane. *The Irresistible Revolution: Living as an Ordinary Radical.* Grand Rapids, MI: Zondervan, 2006.

Evans, Rachel Held. *Inspired: Slaying Giants, Walking on Water and Loving the Bible Again.* Nashville: Thomas Nelson, 2018.

Fields, Karen. "Christian Missionaries as Anticolonial Militants." *Theory and Society* 11, no. 1 (1982): 95–108.

Gilbert, Jack. *Refusing Heaven.* New York: Alfred A. Knopf, 2005.

Heschel, Abraham Joshua. *The Prophets.* New York: Harper Perennial, 2001.

Kegler, Emmy. *One Coin Found: How God's Love Stretches to the Margins*. Minneapolis: Fortress, 2019.

Kroeger, Catherine, and Kroeger, Richard C. *I Suffer Not a Woman: Rethinking 1 Timothy 2:11–15 in Light of Ancient Evidence*. Grand Rapids, MI: Baker Academic, 1981.

Levenson, Jon. *Death and Resurrection of the Beloved Son: The Transformation of Child Sacrifice in Judaism and Christianity*. Binghamton, NY: Yale University Press, 1993.

Mayfield, D. L. *Assimilate or Go Home: Notes from a Failed Missionary on Rediscovering Faith*. San Francisco: HarperOne, 2016.

McKenna, Margaret. "Mark 1: Relocation to Abandoned Places of Empire." In *School(s) for Conversion: 12 Marks of a New Monasticism*, edited by the Rutba House, 10–25. Eugene, OR: Cascade, 2005.

Milgrom, Jacob. *The JPS Torah Commentary: Numbers*. Philadelphia: Jewish Publication Society, 1990.

Olson, Dennis. *Numbers*. Louisville: John Knox, 1996.

Reif, Stephen. "What Enraged Phinehas? A Study of Numbers 25:8." *Journal of Biblical Literature* 90, no. 2 (1971): 200–226.

Sakenfeld, Katharine Doob. "Numbers." In *Women's Bible Commentary*, edited by Carol Newsom, Sharon Ringe, and Jacqueline Lapsley, 79–87. Louisville: Westminster John Knox, 2012.

Schifferdecker, Kathryn. *Out of the Whirlwind: Creation Theology in the Book of Job*. Cambridge, MA: Harvard University Press, 2008.

Trible, Phyllis. "Biblical Views: Wrestling with Faith." *Biblical Archeology Review* 40, no. 5 (September–October 2014). https://www.baslibrary.org/biblical-archaeology-review/40/5/10.

———. *Texts of Terror: Literary-Feminist Readings of Biblical Narratives.* Philadelphia: Fortress, 1983.

Ward, Benedicta, trans. *The Sayings of the Desert Fathers: The Alphabetical Collection.* Kalamazoo, MI: Cistercian, 1975.

West, Cornel. *Race Matters.* Boston: Beacon, 2017.

Westfall, Cynthia Long. *Paul and Gender: Reclaiming the Apostle's Vision for Men and Women in Christ.* Grand Rapids, MI: Baker Academic, 2016.

Wortley, John, trans. *The Book of the Elders: Sayings of the Desert Fathers; The Systematic Collection.* Collegeville, MN: Liturgical Press, 2012.

Zornberg, Avivah Gottlieb. *Bewilderments: Reflections on the Book of Numbers.* New York: Schocken, 2015.

THEOLOGY FOR CHRISTIAN MINISTRY

Informing and inspiring Christian leaders and communities to proclaim God's *Word* to a *World* God created and loves. Articulating the fullness of both realities and the creative intersection between them.

Word & World Books is a partnership between Luther Seminary, the board of the periodical *Word & World*, and Fortress Press.

Books in the series include:

Future Faith: Ten Challenges Reshaping Christianity in the 21st Century by Wesley Granberg-Michaelson (2018)

Liberating Youth from Adolescence by Jeremy P. Myers (2018)

Elders Rising: The Promise and Peril of Aging by Roland Martinson (2018)

I Can Do No Other: The Church's New Here We Stand Moment by Anna M. Madsen (2019)

Intercultural Church: A Biblical Vision for an Age of Migration by Safwat Marzouk (2019)

Rooted and Renewing: Imagining the Church's Future in Light of Its New Testament Origins by Troy M. Troftgruben (2019)

Journeying in the Wilderness: Forming Faith in the 21st Century by Terri Martinson Elton (2020)

God So Enters into Relationships That . . . : A Biblical View by Terence E. Fretheim (2020)

Today Everything Is Different: An Adventure in Prayer and Action by Dirk G. Lange (2021)

Life Unsettled: A Scriptural Journey for Wilderness Times by Cory Driver (2021)